What Cancer Taught Me

A Memoir

By Sue Straus

Dedicated to Grandma Dena, Lani and Valerie, and all the warriors out there

To Grandma Dena: I have never met anyone like you. You were able to turn even the most dreadful tasks (like cleaning my room) into a game and make them fun. You made me laugh so hard my stomach hurt. Everyone who knew you loved you. You fought hard against cancer, but unfortunately lost the battle. You are my inspiration and because of you, I hope to be an inspiration to others. My time with you was wonderful, but way too short! Not a day goes by that I don't miss you!

To Lani and Valerie: I love you more than words can express. You make me so proud because of all of your accomplishments and the truly wonderful women you have become. I am honored to call myself both your mother and your friend. I hope I inspire you to continue to do great things and to continue to be the fantastic women you are.

To all the warriors out there: Stay strong, stay positive, and remember, you are not alone!

Table of Contents

Introduction

I was born on June 2, 1960. Although I was full term, I only weighed four pounds, four ounces. I had to stay in the hospital in an incubator for one month. Doctors assured my parents that there was no cause for concern and I would have no health issues. I even surprised everyone because most babies lose a few pounds after they are born, but I never lost any. After one month, I left the hospital weighing five pounds, five and a half ounces. But this is not a memoir about my birth or childhood. This is about cancer.

My first experiences with cancer were when my grandparents were diagnosed with it. They were both in their seventies, so I thought cancer was a disease of the elderly. I never expected to be diagnosed at age thirty-four. So that is when my cancer journey began and where this story begins. I have been diagnosed and treated for cancer four times! After reading that sentence, you might be thinking that I must feel like the unluckiest person in the world. Therefore, it will most likely surprise you to know that I don't. I actually feel quite lucky. You see, cancer has taught me some things that I might never have learned if I never had cancer.

I have divided this book into two parts. The first part describes my diagnoses and treatments. The second part explains what cancer has taught me.

Part 1

Cancer #1 Thyroid Cancer

"Oh no, not tonsillitis again!" That was my first thought on a Thursday night in December of 1993 when I felt a sudden sharp pain in my throat. My two daughters (Ilana, who we have called Lani since she was about eight months old, was three years old, and Valerie, who was five months old) were in bed. I was working at my desk in the kitchen on lesson plans for my second grade class, and suddenly I was startled by the stinging in my throat.

I had begun my teaching career in 1984. Every year for the first five years, I would develop tonsillitis which consisted of a high fever and terrible sore throat that lasted for about a week. I was tested for strep each time, and the result was always negative. After the fifth time, my doctor stated that if I contracted it again, he wanted to take out my tonsils. I used to joke that he scared the tonsillitis out of me because I never became infected with it again after he said that.

So, after feeling that piercing ache, I reached up and under the neck of my turtleneck to see if the glands in my neck felt swollen. I thought I felt a lump on the right side, so I went to the bathroom to look in the mirror. I was horrified to see a noticeable bulge. I thought I must be imagining it because I was worried about getting tonsillitis again, even though it had been years. I decided to ask my husband. (Note: my husband and I separated in 2015, but I will get to that later).

I left the bathroom and walked into the office off the family room where my husband was working on something. I pulled the neck of my turtleneck down and started to ask, "Do you see anything on my neck?" Before I could finish my sentence, he exclaimed loudly, "What is that?" and pointed to my neck. I guess I wasn't imagining anything. Seeing as it was Thursday evening, I planned to call my doctor first thing in the morning to try to get an appointment on Friday.

When I had a break from teaching Friday morning, I went to make the call. I wanted to speak in private. All of the phones, except for one, were in open areas where anyone could overhear the conversation. The only phone that was totally private was in a closet! Even though it was somewhat cramped and awkward to talk in a closet, I went to that phone because I didn't want to have any of the other staff members overhear and start asking me what was wrong. Unfortunately, I was told by the receptionist that I could not be squeezed in that day, and that the earliest the doctor could see me was next Tuesday. My insistent pleading did not faze her or change the outcome. I was extremely frustrated and discouraged because I had to wait the whole weekend! Thus commenced the first of many times waiting for medical results.

I have decided that waiting for medical results is worse than receiving a horrible diagnosis! Fear of the unknown is a terrible thing. Your mind goes wild and imagines unthinkable things and worst-case scenarios. When you get a diagnosis, even if it is not the one you were hoping for, at least you know what you are dealing with and can plan a course of action.

So, four long days later, I visited my doctor. He performed the usual examination – listened to my heart, my lungs, took my blood pressure, and looked in my eyes, ears, and throat. Then he filled a small plastic cup with water and handed it to me. I said, "Thanks, but I'm not really thirsty." I was still unsettled about the swelling in my neck, too nervous to drink. He laughed and replied that he wanted to examine my thyroid and that the easiest way to do that was to feel it when I swallowed. He explained that most people find it easier to swallow when they are sipping on water. Oops! I had no idea! So, I sipped and he palpated my neck a few times. He informed me that it was definitely my thyroid, and he suggested I follow up with an endocrinologist.

I scheduled an appointment with an endocrinologist, Dr. D, about a week later. Dr. D examined me with the same cup of water and swallow technique. He also drew blood. All of my bloodwork was normal, so even with this mysterious mass, my thyroid was functioning normally. He pronounced that he was pleased about that, but he wanted to do further testing, specifically, a radioactive iodine scan. He explained that the thyroid attracts iodine so I would swallow a pill that contains a small amount of radioactive iodine. I would then have a scan of my neck, and the radioactive iodine would make the thyroid much easier to see. The scan had to be performed in a special section of a hospital because precautions were necessary when using radiation. Luckily, it was painless, similar to having an x-ray, and after completing it one morning, I was able to return to school to teach my class in the afternoon. When I arrived at school, I jokingly asked the secretary, "Am I glowing?" It's a very small amount of radiation, but we laughed.

Dr. D called later that day and reported that I had two nodules on my thyroid. There was a large nodule of over two centimeters (the one that was noticeably visible) that was called a hot nodule and another nodule that was only a few millimeters in size that was called a cold nodule. Hot nodules are usually benign and can be fluid-filled (which mine was) and cold nodules are usually solid and can be malignant. He recommended that the nodules be biopsied and referred me to an endocrine surgeon with a long Italian name starting with the letter G. My husband could never remember his name and called him Dr. Guacamole. I will respectfully refer to him as Dr. G.

I scheduled the appointment at Dr. G's first availability and arranged for a substitute for my class. It was an early morning appointment a few days later. Dr. G sat me in a chair that was similar to those in a dentist's office. Out of the corner of my eye, I glimpsed what looked like a syringe and watched him bring it toward my neck. It was a little alarming to see that! It was quite painful as he extracted a large amount of fluid from my neck. He assured me that he would call me as soon as he had the results. I was feeling very sore, so I called school and arranged for the sub to stay for the rest of the day, and I went home. Even though I was uncomfortable, I was pleased to note that by extracting all of the fluid, the bulge in my neck was no longer visible.

About a week later, Dr. D telephoned. He said that he had received the report from the biopsy that Dr. G performed. The large fluid filled nodule was benign. Phew! What a relief! But then he mentioned that there is a twenty-five percent false benign rate! Twenty-five percent!! That seemed too high. He also stated that because the smaller nodule was deep within my neck, it was not able to be biopsied. He decided that the best course of action was to start me on a medication called Synthroid. Synthroid is a synthetic substitute of the hormone produced by the thyroid. The thinking was that I would absorb all of the hormone from the medicine so my thyroid would not have to do any work. By making it so that my thyroid was inactive, both nodules should shrink. Okay, that sounded like a good plan.

So for approximately the entire next year, I was taking decreasing doses of Synthroid. I started on a small amount and then had my blood tested after six to eight weeks because it takes the body at least six weeks to adjust to changes in Synthroid doses. After the first check, Dr. D said that the thyroid hormone level was too high and switched me to a lower dose. I again had my blood drawn after six to eight weeks. The hormone level was still too high, so I was given an even lower dose. After about a year of this continued pattern, the hormone level remained too high, and there was not a lower dose of Synthroid available. Another scan of my thyroid was performed to see if the nodules had shrunk, and sadly, they looked to be about the same size. Dr. D felt that surgery to remove my thyroid was the next step. Needless to say, I was anxious and scared. I had never had major surgery before.

The surgery was scheduled with Dr. G for the Monday before Christmas in December of 1994. It was an early morning surgery, and I had to be at the hospital at 6:30 in the morning! My daughters were ages four and one then, and I usually took them to daycare at 7:45. How was my husband going to get me to the hospital by 6:30 and them to daycare at 7:45? We certainly couldn't leave them alone at home while he took me to the hospital! If we brought them in the car for the ride to the hospital, he could drop me off, take them to daycare afterwards, and then come back to the hospital to be with me until it was time to pick them up again. However, it was very early for them to get up and more time than I wanted for them to be in the car. I was stressing about it and mentioned it to my daycare provider, Kaye. Kaye offered to watch them, indicating that we could drop them off at her house on the way to the hospital. She suggested we bring them to her in their pajamas and supply a change of clothes for them. She would dress and feed them, and my husband could stay with me at the hospital. Then he could come back between 4:00 and 5:00 in the evening to pick them up as usual. Kaye's idea was wonderful! One less thing to worry about.

Dr. G explained the surgery to me. He informed me that the surgery would take about three hours, I would be intubated, and the entire thyroid would be removed. He mentioned that because the thyroid is in a slightly different place in every person, depending on how easy or difficult it was to remove, I might need drainage tubes in my neck afterwards. I found it strange that the thyroid isn't in the same spot in everyone. I thought all body parts were located in the same place in every person! I guess this is another tidbit of information cancer taught me! I would need to stay overnight in the hospital, but it was expected that I would be able to go home the following day. Since it was the week before Christmas, I would take leave for that whole week and have the following week off as well due to the holiday. Dr. G assured me that as soon as the holiday was over, I would be able to return to work.

When I woke up from the surgery, I was thrilled to discover that I didn't need drainage tubes because my recovery would be easier without them. My throat was sore from the intubation tube, but otherwise, I really didn't have much discomfort. I spent a relatively pain-free and uneventful night in the hospital. The next day though, I felt very odd. The only way I can describe it is that I felt like a caged animal. I felt like I had to pace. I couldn't sit still or lie in bed. Dr. G had remarked that one of my parathyroid glands had turned dusky gray during the surgery because it wasn't getting enough blood supply, but he expected it to return to normal functioning soon after the surgery. I think the agitated feeling I had was related to a change in the parathyroid function, but I can't be sure. The feeling only lasted about twenty-four hours, and I've never experienced it again since.

About three days after surgery, Dr. D called. He had received the pathology report from the hospital. He informed me that the fluid filled nodule was indeed benign but that the smaller solid mass was malignant! I was shocked! I was only thirty-four years old. I never expected to be diagnosed with cancer at age thirty-four! The good news was that the tumor was only seven millimeters in size. Dr. D explained that anything under one centimeter was considered non-life threatening and that there was no further treatment needed! Yay! So, I went back to work in January.

I remember noticing that my voice was extremely hoarse. At the end of the day, it was so gravelly that I would call myself Kim Carnes, the singer with the very raspy voice! Then one day in the first week back at school, I was sitting at the kidney bean shaped table conducting reading groups. While I was leading one group, the other children had work to do at their seats before going to centers they were assigned to each day. As one of the students in my group was reading aloud, I heard a bit of a commotion in the back of the room. I glanced up from the table and saw a student trying to join in at a center different from the one he had been assigned to for that day. The students at the center were attempting to shoo him away. I tried to raise my voice to instruct him to go to his assigned center, and nothing came out. It was like my most scary recurring nightmare. I have a nightmare where

I am in danger and no matter how hard I try to scream, no sound comes out of my mouth! I attempted to remain calm and not worry about my voice, trying to convince myself it was part of the healing process after surgery. I decided I would ignore it the best I could and wait to discuss it with Dr. G at my post-surgery appointment scheduled in a couple weeks.

When I went for the post-surgery appointment, Dr. G looked at my scar and remarked that I was healing quite nicely. It is a very long scar, about five inches long, as if he had literally slit my throat. Even though it is so long, he positioned it so that it aligns with a natural wrinkle in my neck. To this day, unless you peer very closely, and know what you are looking for, you would not notice the scar. The only follow-up is that I have to continue to take Synthroid for the rest of my life, and I need to have bloodwork performed every six months to make sure the dose is correct. I mentioned my raspy voice to Dr. G and explained that the louder I tried to talk, the less volume came out of my mouth. It didn't seem to be improving. He informed me that there are two nerves that feed the vocal chords. In my case, my thyroid was growing around one of those nerves so that when he removed it, there was some damage to the nerve. Really?! He didn't tell me! Would he have mentioned it if I hadn't expressed my concerns about my voice?

Dr. G referred me to a woman who worked in the hospital near my house and conducted voice therapy. I took a month leave from teaching. I was advised to limit my speaking each day and meet with her twice a week. Telling a woman to limit her talking is a harsh punishment! I used to chat with my best friend, Betsy, every day, and now I wouldn't be able to speak with her much for a whole month. That was challenging, but I wanted to save the little bit that I was allowed to talk each day for conversations with my husband and children. The therapist also gave me exercises to do at home. The exercises were peculiar. I was instructed to make these almost animal sounding grunting noises to exercise the vocal chords. I felt very self-conscious and only practiced them when no one was around. It was sort of a surreal experience because I was on sick-leave from work for a month, but I felt fine. I slept in and took my daughters to daycare an hour later than usual for that whole month. While they were at daycare and my husband was at work, I dutifully performed my voice exercises, read, took an exercise class, cooked some meals to freeze for when I went back to work, and had a relaxing month. I did feel a little guilty for using leave when I wasn't sick. I've never been one to play hooky or shirk my duties. Toward the end of the month, however, I was almost in tears. I voiced my disappointment to my husband saying that although I had done everything I had been told (limited my talking, vocal exercises at home, etc.), there was no improvement. It was as if my prayers were answered because the very next day I noticed my voice was less raspy and I was able to project more! Goodbye Kim Carnes and welcome back Sue Straus! From that day on, my voice gradually improved until it returned to normal. So, the month ended, and I went back to work feeling like my old self again.

I did have a run-in with Kaye, my daycare provider though. At the end of the month, she handed me a bill to pay extra for that month. I don't remember the exact amount, but I do remember that it was substantial, on top of what I already paid her each month for childcare. She stated it was to cover supervising my daughters for that extra hour and a half on the day of my surgery. I couldn't believe it! I reminded her that she had offered to take them. I hadn't asked her. She offered! I also emphasized that because I had brought them an hour later than usual for a whole month, she had to care for them less and that it more than made up for that early hour and a half. She responded that it was her policy to charge extra for early drop off or late pick up. I was so insulted! It wasn't as if I was using her and going shopping or something frivolous while she had to spend extra time watching my daughters. I paid her and admitted that I wished she would have let me know upfront that she would be charging me extra. I probably would have still had her take them, but it wouldn't have stung so much if I had known ahead of time. I felt that this situation changed our relationship and left a bad taste in my mouth. I wanted the woman who was taking care of my children to be someone I had implicit faith in and felt wonderful about in every way, and I no longer felt that way about Kaye. I searched for a new daycare provider and switched my daughters later that year. From the start, I loved the new daycare provider, and I was happy. So, life went on.

Cancer #2 Breast Cancer

In 2005, I decided I wanted a change in my career. I had been teaching elementary school for over twenty years, mostly second grade. I had a master's degree in mathematics education, and I wanted to teach some higher level math classes. I decided to switch to middle school. My own daughters were in middle school and high school, so I felt I could relate to students that age. Also, the start time for elementary school is different from the start time for middle school where I teach. I used to say goodbye to my daughters in the morning as they left for school and still have close to an hour before I had to leave the house to go to my school. Then I would still be teaching in the afternoon and would realize that as I was standing in my classroom, my daughters were already home from school. I thought that if I switched to middle school, my schedule would be closer to theirs. If you would have asked me at the beginning of my teaching career if I would have considered teaching middle school, I would have exclaimed, "Are you out of your mind?" It is a difficult age, but in 2005 I felt I was up for the challenge.

I ended up transferring to a school that I hadn't expected. I was used to driving only about five minutes to get to my elementary school, so I was considering middle schools that were all within a fifteen minute drive from home. Unfortunately, there were no openings. A school that was about a half an hour away (without traffic!) advertised a math position.

I set up an interview and was extremely impressed with the principal. She asked the usual questions about my discipline style, how I structure a typical lesson, what I do to help struggling students, and how I enrich the students who understand the material. Then she posed a question I had never been asked on an interview before. She said, "If you posted a sign in your classroom that was your motto or philosophy of teaching, what would it say?" I thought for a moment and then replied that I really had two. "Respect yourself, others, and your school" would be one. I am a firm believer that respect is one of the most important qualities, if not THE most important trait a person can possess and demonstrate to others. I did end up posting a sign to list the rules for my classroom with "Respect yourself, others, and your school!" on it. I put "Do your homework" under the "Respect Yourself" category, and "Keep your hands and feet to yourself" under the "Respect Others" category, just to name a few. The other sign would read, "Never stop learning!" I believe there are always new things to learn, and I enjoy learning them. Hence the title of this memoir! After the formal interview, she guided me on a tour of the building. We were standing in the hallway when the bell rang for students to switch classes. Students began approaching the principal, hugging her, and sharing good grades they had received. I was mightily impressed! Middle schoolers are a tough group who don't open up easily. For them to seem this close to the principal made me think that it would be wonderful to work with her. Before I left home for the interview, I had said to my husband that I was going for the interview experience but not because I wanted to work there. When I got home, I surprised him by informing him that I would take the job if she offered it to me and that I hoped she did. On June 2nd, my birthday, she called and offered me the position. I think it was a good sign that I got the job on my birthday. Everything was great for the first year at my new school.

The Saturday before Thanksgiving in 2006 (my second year at the middle school), my husband and I went bowling with another couple. It had been years since I had been bowling, and I had a wonderful time. When we got home, I grabbed my pajamas and proceeded into the bathroom to change. Usually I would change in the closet because we had a big walk-in closet and the laundry basket was in there. I could change and throw the dirty clothes right in the basket. I have no idea why I went into the bathroom instead of changing in the closet, but I am so glad I did! As I was undressing in front of the mirror, I noticed that my left breast appeared to be sagging. It didn't resemble my right breast. I know they aren't symmetrical or identical, but it looked remarkably different. Just as I had with the lump in my neck, my first thought was that I was imagining it. Why do I always think that? Is it human nature or just me? I guess no one wants to find out they have something seriously wrong. In any case, I called my husband to take a look. I didn't want to tell him what I had observed and guide him to the same conclusion. I wanted to find out if he would determine anything on his own, so I just asked him if he noticed anything about my left breast. He claimed it looked like it was sagging a little more than the right one. Okay, once again, I was not imagining it!

First thing the next morning, I called my primary care physician. She informed me that she could squeeze me in that afternoon. She gave me an appointment at a time that allowed me to teach the whole day and then go to her office. I was glad I didn't need to procure a sub. I put it out of my mind and went to school. At the end of the day, I drove to her office. Surprisingly, I was not feeling nervous because I had had a mammogram about six months earlier and it had been normal. She performed a full breast exam on both breasts and stared at both of them for a long time. She said, "This doesn't look the way breast cancer usually does, but I'd recommend you have a diagnostic mammogram and ultrasound." Even though I had had a mammogram less than a year ago, she wanted me to have another one because of the change in appearance, and a diagnostic mammogram consists of more views than a routine mammogram. She reassured me that having both scans would definitely reveal what was there, if anything. I was able to get an appointment at a nearby radiology center for the next morning and arranged for a substitute.

The mammogram didn't seem to be any different from all the previous ones I had except that there were four views taken of each breast instead of two. Afterwards, the woman who had performed the mammogram ushered me down a hallway to have the ultrasound. From my position on the bed/table, I could see the screen with the image of my breast as the ultrasound was happening. I noticed several times that the sonographer was marking the distance between two points on the screen and measuring the distance. I knew this was not a good sign.

In 2000, I had had severe pains during the first two days of my menstrual cycle. My gynecologist had felt a mass on my right ovary. He sent me for an ultrasound and a cyst was discovered. I remember that sonographer measuring it the same way this sonographer was doing to my breast. I needed to have my right ovary removed because it was a large cyst causing considerable discomfort. Thankfully, it was not cancer but something called a dermoid cyst. It's a cyst that can have teeth and hair growing in it! Gross!

So here I was thinking I have something growing in my breast, but not panicking yet. Any woman who has ever had a mammogram knows that afterwards the technician asks you to wait as the radiologist reads the films to make sure the views are clear. If everything looks clear in a readable sense, not necessarily clear of growths, the technician comes back and tells you that you are free to go. If anything is blurry, the technician comes back and tells you more views need to be taken. So, the sonographer had me wait in the room outside of where she had just performed the ultrasound while she went to show the results to the pathologist. I sat there apprehensively awaiting her return, worrying that she would tell me something was wrong. I wasn't sure if I would know anything that day or if I had to wait several days for my doctor to call with the results. She returned a few minutes later, asked me to get dressed, and added that the pathologist wanted to speak to me. I knew it! I had something in my left breast. Well, at least I was finding out right away!

I got dressed and followed the woman as she led me to the room where the pathologist reads all of the x-rays, ultrasounds, etc. I entered the room and saw views of my breast posted all around! Wow! Embarrassing! Even more embarrassing was the fact that this pathologist was a very young and good looking man! He pointed to one view of my breast that contained a round shadow. He stated that it was a tumor that seemed to be about eight millimeters. He explained that in this view it appeared to have uniform edges which usually means that it is benign. But then he showed me another view where the edges looked uneven. He claimed that this could mean cancer. His recommendation was that I have it biopsied. He suggested I contact my doctor for the name of a breast surgeon to do the biopsy. I thanked him and left in a daze. I staggered through the parking lot to my car and tried not to cry.

When I returned home, my husband was working in the office off the family room. At that time he had a job where he worked from home. It was about 11:00 in the morning, and he was on a business call. I walked into the office and sat down on a chair to wait for him to finish his call. After he hung up, he turned to me and started ranting about the phone call. I have no idea what he said. In the middle of his tirade, I interrupted him and exclaimed, "They saw a lump on the ultrasound." He instantly stopped talking and the look on his face became serious. Then he questioned, "What happens now?" I responded that my doctor was going to call and provide me with the name of a breast surgeon to do a biopsy. I added that I didn't know much but had been thinking on the short trip home. I had decided that if it was cancer and I needed to have a mastectomy, I wanted to have reconstructive surgery. He asked, "How do they do that? Do they stuff it with cotton?" I stared at him incredulously and then stormed up to our bedroom to be alone.

One thing cancer taught me (no, I am not saving this for part two) is that most people are genuinely kind and good-hearted. They often don't know the right thing to say. They come across as unfeeling or uncaring because they either say nothing for fear of saying the wrong thing, or actually say the wrong thing thinking that they are helping. This came up many times in my cancer journey.

So in my husband's case, he came across as extremely insensitive. I was shocked and hurt. He later apologized and explained that he was so blown away by my news that he tried to inject levity thinking it would help and as a sort of defense mechanism for his own fear. It is not how I would have reacted had the tables been turned, but I accepted his apology.

Later that afternoon, my doctor called and gave me the name of two breast surgeons. Because it was now the Tuesday before Thanksgiving, it was a little difficult to schedule an appointment. Many doctors' offices were going to be closed Thursday and Friday. The first surgeon I called reported that he couldn't see me for three weeks! I knew the stress of waiting three weeks would be too much. I called the other surgeon and she was able to arrange an appointment on the Monday after Thanksgiving.

Even though everyone in my family (my parents, both of my sisters, both of my brothers-in-law, my husband) and I all matriculated from the University of Wisconsin in Madison, we all ended up in Maryland. Well, all except my parents, but my sisters and I are working on that! What brought me to Maryland and made me leave my hometown of Milwaukee? My sisters did. My oldest sister, Jill, met her husband, Andy, in college. Andy grew up in Maryland, and a few years after they got married, he convinced Jill to move back there with him. My middle sister, Lori, met her husband, Gary, at Andy and Jill's wedding. It turns out that Gary and Andy were childhood friends. It's wonderful that not only are they best friends, but now they are brothers-in-law too. After Lori and Gary had been married for a few years, they also decided to relocate to Maryland. I had graduated from college in 1982 and a year later was living in an apartment with my friend Beth who later became my maid-of-honor. I was working as a bank teller because it was nearly impossible to secure a teaching job in Milwaukee. Vacancies only occurred when someone died or retired! In the spring of 1983, Jill and Lori each had their first child, girls for both. They would send frequent pictures. I was thinking about how my nieces would grow up and wouldn't know their Aunt Sue because I lived so far away. Also, I wasn't getting a teaching job. So, what was holding me to

Milwaukee? Not much! I decided to move to Maryland in 1984.

Now every year on Thanksgiving, since my sisters and I are all in Maryland, my parents come to visit. They repeatedly say how lucky they are to have all three children in one place and not spread across the country like many of their friends. They usually come on the Wednesday before Thanksgiving. They stay at Jill's house on Wednesday night since she hosts the Thanksgiving meal, and my mother likes to be there to help Jill prepare everything. Then they spend a night or two at Lori's and a night or two at my house. That way they can spend individual time with each of the grandkids.

Thursday afternoon, I drove to meet my parents and my sisters at Jill's house before Gary joined us with his kids and my husband brought our kids. I told them I wanted to discuss something with them. I described the events leading up to that day. I reported that I had noticed a change in the shape of my left breast and that while the mammogram showed nothing, a spot was discovered on the ultrasound. I informed them that I was scheduled to have it biopsied on Monday, but I had decided not to mention anything to my kids yet. I explained that even though they were sixteen and thirteen years old, I didn't want to worry them if it turned out to be nothing. If it was identified as cancer, then I would inform them. I wanted them to be able to concentrate on school and their own lives without worrying about mine.

On Monday morning, my husband and my parents accompanied me to meet Dr. W, the breast surgeon. She explained that she would be performing an ultrasound guided biopsy. While my family waited in the waiting room, I was instructed to put on a paper gown and then was led to the exam room. Dr. W injected my breast with four shots of a local numbing agent. She informed me that the tumor was very deep, a few centimeters from the chest wall, which was why it hadn't been visible on the mammogram. She claimed that to get the best angle, she was going to have to inject the needle close to my nipple to do the biopsy. When I heard that, I thought, "Ow! That is really going to hurt a lot!" Thankfully, the numbing agent worked well. I felt a little pain, but mostly just pressure as she put the needle in and took it out about six times. She was very kind, frequently asking me if I was okay or feeling any pain. When she finished, Dr. W indicated that she would probably have the results by Wednesday. I was relieved. Two days wasn't too long to wait for results.

However, that was not the case. Again, I began a long wait for test results. Wednesday came and went, and there was no word from Dr. W. I was beginning to feel very anxious. My sisters and parents kept calling to ask if I had heard anything. I know they were worried too, but that made me even more anxious! By Thursday, I was so nervous that I drove to school and left my purse at home! That meant I was driving without having my driver's license with me! I had never driven anywhere without my driver's license before! My school had been on a block schedule which meant that classes were ninety minutes long. I taught my first block and had the next block free. I used the free block to drive home, get my purse, and drive all the way back to school again! I just didn't like the idea of not having it with me. Then I taught my last block of the day and was feeling so distraught, I arranged for a substitute to cover my classes on Friday. I still had to wait anxiously all day Friday to hear the results because Dr. W didn't call until 4:30 in the afternoon! She told me that the pathologist didn't see cancer cells outright but he saw some abnormal cells. He was going to reread the slides on Monday and have another pathologist give his opinion as well. Dr. W felt that since cancer cells could be right next to abnormal cells, she wanted to perform a lumpectomy and remove the tumor. By removing it, it could be biopsied to ensure an exact diagnosis. That sounded like an excellent plan. Dr. W scheduled the surgery for December 15, 2006. I would take leave from work from December 15th through the rest of the month and go back to work in January after the winter break. It was the same plan as when I had my thyroidectomy – surgery the week before the winter break and then back to work after the winter break. Dr. W promised that she would call me Monday and report the pathologist's conclusion.

On Monday morning, I went to speak with my principal. Unfortunately, the principal who had hired me the year before had been involuntarily transferred to a high school over the summer after my first year of working with her, and my school was assigned a new principal who had been hired from another state. He didn't really know me at all, and he wasn't aware of my teaching record with the county. I emphasized that I wanted to be honest and upfront with him. I explained that as of now I was scheduled for surgery on the fifteenth. If my tumor was benign, I would be back at school after winter break. If it was malignant, I would let him know when I would return once I was informed of the plan. He thanked me for sharing what was happening and wished me good luck and good news.

Later that afternoon, as I was in the middle of teaching a class, another teacher walked into my room and informed me that she was going to cover my class while I took a call. She stated that my husband was on the phone. When I picked up the receiver, my husband announced that Dr. W had called. I asked him what she told him, and his words were, "You know what she said." We had both kind of expected her to call back and report that it was cancer. I replied that I was going to make sure my classes were covered for the rest of the day and come home. He instructed me come to Dr. W's office because she had suggested we both come there to discuss the next steps. He asked if I would be okay driving. I assured him that I would be and responded that I would meet him there. That day was December 4, 2006. I will always remember that that was the date I was diagnosed with breast cancer.

As Dr. W ushered us into an exam room, she handed me a large binder. She informed me that it was filled with all kinds of useful information about breast cancer. I still have that binder. I have read it cover to cover, and it has been a wealth of information! Dr. W proceeded to describe the next step which was for me to receive a breast MRI. She explained that the purpose of the MRI was to make sure that there were no other tumors in the breast with the mass or in the other breast before she performed the surgery. If there were no other growths, surgery would be as scheduled on December 15th.

That night, my husband and I sat our daughters down at the kitchen table to explain to them what was happening. Even though Lani was sixteen and Valerie was thirteen at that time, and we knew they were old enough to understand, I'm glad we had decided to wait until we knew the results before sharing them. Nevertheless, it was one of the most difficult conversations I have ever had. As a mom, you never want to say anything that will hurt your children. We briefly described the events leading up to that day. The minute we used the word cancer, they both started to cry. That choked me up! We discussed the fact that the tumor was small which gave me an excellent prognosis. Lani asked why we hadn't told them sooner and seemed a little upset that we hadn't. I explained that I had wanted their main focus to be on school and maintaining their good grades. I didn't want them to worry if it had turned out to be benign. We ended the conversation with hugs, and I hoped that they weren't too worried about me.

I had only planned to miss work right before my surgery, but ended up taking leave for the rest of December. The MRI revealed another tumor. I returned to Dr. W to have that one biopsied. Before she started, she explained that it was located in a different quadrant in the breast from the original tumor. If it had been in the same quadrant, I could have a lumpectomy, but since it was not, I would have to have a mastectomy. Then she started the ultrasound to find the tumor to biopsy it. It was gone! She remarked that many women have hormonal changes in their breasts due to their menstrual cycles and that something visible one day might not be seen the next. That would mean that it definitely was not cancer. So this new tumor was not cancer. Hooray for some positive news! Thankfully, I didn't have a second biopsy and I could have a lumpectomy. Dr. W then described my options. If I had a lumpectomy, she would remove the tumor and some tissue around it to get clear margins verifying that all of the cancer had been removed. I would then need six and a half weeks of radiation. The advantage is I would still have my own breast. If I had a mastectomy, she would remove my whole breast, and follow-up radiation wouldn't be necessary. I could choose to have reconstruction at a later date if I wanted it. I asked her if there was a greater chance of recurrence with either one. She assured me that the prognosis and outcome of both were the same. I decided I wanted to keep my breast. I was only forty-six!

Dr. W described the details of a lumpectomy. Not only would she remove the tumor, but she would extract several lymph nodes as well to determine whether or not they contained any cancer cells. If there were cancer cells visible in the lymph nodes, there was a possibility that the cancer had metastasized elsewhere in my body. If there were no cancer cells discovered in the lymph nodes, it would mean that the cancer was limited to my breast. Obviously, I was praying that there were no cancer cells in the lymph nodes! When you get a cancer diagnosis, it's bad news. After that, you keep hoping for the best bad news – kind of like a best case scenario given the situation.

Dr. W performs surgery at a surgi-center. I needed to be there early on the morning of December 15th. I was directed to pre-op where a nurse instructed me to change into a cloth hospital gown and checked my vital signs: temperature, blood pressure (which I'm sure was extremely high due to nerves, even though I don't remember), etc. Then she explained that I was going to be sent for another mammogram. While my breast was being smushed between the plates, the radiologist was going to insert a wire into it to mark the spot of the tumor. This would guide Dr. W as she did the lumpectomy.

I rode the elevator up to the waiting room to await my mammogram. I was dressed in the clothes I came in wearing from the waist down, but I was clad in just the cloth gown on top. As I sat in the waiting room, I observed that it was filled with women donning paper gowns and awaiting their annual mammograms. Two women were sitting near me and chatting as if they were old friends. At one point, I heard one of them say to the other while motioning in my direction, "I wish I could have a cloth gown like she has instead of this paper one." I became incensed! I was already so nervous and stressed about my diagnosis and imminent surgery that I almost blurted out, "Would you like the breast cancer that goes with it?" I bit back the caustic retort and remained quiet. I acted like I didn't hear her, although I was probably visibly shaking because I was so angry! Later, when I took a moment to think about it and calm down, I remembered what I had learned about people and how most are not intentionally mean and insensitive. She wasn't trying to be either of those. She didn't know my situation. I'm glad I didn't respond to her!

After the guidewire was inserted, I trekked back downstairs. The nurse instructed me to finish undressing and started my IV with a saline drip. She informed me that a doctor would be injecting my breast with dye so that when my lymph nodes were checked, the pathologist would be able to see if they contained any cancer. After the injection of the dye, I would be wheeled into the surgical suite, Dr. W would meet me in there with the anesthesiologist, and my surgery would begin. I don't remember how long she said it would last or if they had to intubate me for this surgery.

I was wheeled into a room where a male doctor was waiting for me so that he could inject me with the dye. He explained that he would give me four shots to numb my breast and then four shots with the dye. They were given around my breast as if it were a compass: at north, south, east, and west. First came the numbing shots – ouch! They hurt like hell!!!!! I think I have a high tolerance for pain, but those numbing shots rank up there as the second most excruciating experience I've ever had (the most painful experience being when I passed a kidney stone) – even worse than when I had the biopsy for my thyroid tumor! Supposedly my breast was now numb, so he could administer the shots for the dye. Ouch! That still stung! It wasn't quite as bad as the numbing shots, but it was still awful. I was wishing the pre-op nurse would have injected something more than just saline in my IV at this point!

Next, I was wheeled into the operating suite. Dr. W greeted me, confirmed that the guidewire was in place, and told me to relax. The anesthesiologist stated that he was going to start injecting medicine in my IV to induce sleep. I remember looking up at the bright lights overhead. They became blurry, and I felt a little woozy. The next thing I knew, I was in a room that looked like the pre-op room and my husband was seated in a chair next to my bed.

The first words out of my mouth were, "Is it in the lymph nodes?" My husband smiled and replied that it was not. Yay! I got the best bad news!!!! "We have to tell Betsy," I said. I noticed he had a weird look on his face. When I asked him what was wrong, he claimed that I had said the exact same thing twice before. What???? I didn't remember anything since being wheeled into the operating room. I guess the anesthesia worked remarkably well!

Then the nurse came by and directed me to drink some ginger ale and eat some saltines. She commented that after I finished eating and drinking, I could get dressed and go home. Surprisingly, I had very little pain. The nurse insisted on giving me a strong analgesic. I think it was Oxycodone. I tried to convince her that I didn't need it. I almost never take pain medications. I have to have a raging headache or a high fever (fortunately I rarely get either) to take pain medication. All I ever take is extra strength Tylenol. I remember when they gave me Oxycodone or something similar in the hospital after my thyroidectomy, it made me sick to my stomach. I explained to the nurse that the Oxycodone would make me nauseous, and I didn't want it, but she insisted. Begrudgingly, I took the pill and got dressed. Then the nurse wheeled me out of the surgi-center to meet my husband who had gone to get the car.

Sure enough, on the way home, I started feeling progressively nauseous. When we were about five minutes from the house, I rolled down the window to get some air. It was December, freezing cold, but I needed air. Also, if I threw up, I could do it out the window. I made it home without throwing up, but I still felt extremely nauseous. I stumbled into the house, through the kitchen, and made my way to my bedroom where I was going to rest. Lani and Valerie had been standing in the kitchen anxiously waiting for me to arrive and to ascertain how I was feeling. I assured them that although I was a little nauseous from the pain medication, otherwise I felt fine and just wanted to lie down in bed. I didn't know it at the time but found out later that they both had taken one look at me and had become stricken. They asked their father what was wrong with me because they had never seen me, or anyone else for that matter, look that way. I was actually green! To this day, Lani insists she will never forget how I looked.

My husband came up to check on me, and I announced that I was going to go to the bathroom.

He said he would wait outside the door just to make sure that I was okay. I repeated that I was fine. I just needed to pee and it wasn't necessary for him to do that, but he insisted. As I stood up to flush the toilet, I looked inside it and burst out laughing. My husband heard me and yelled through the door, "Are you okay?" I answered, "I'm fine, but you have to come in here and see this!" He replied that he didn't want to, but I insisted. He reluctantly opened the door, and I pointed at the toilet. My pee was blue! It looked like I had just cleaned the toilet with Tidy Bowl! We both laughed. I assumed that the dye that they had used in my lymph nodes was blue. When I shared that thought with him, he agreed.

My mother had come to visit and to assist me for the next week while I recuperated. She had slept at one of my sister's houses the night before. After I was resting in bed, she and both of my sisters came over. They brought dinner for all of us. I was still feeling a tad nauseous, so I didn't eat much. By the next day, however, my appetite was back. I had very little discomfort and didn't take any more of the prescription pain medication. I think that also helped my appetite.

I was wrapped in gauze and tape. There was an incision in my breast from where Dr. W performed the lumpectomy, and another one in my armpit from where she had removed the lymph nodes. Both dressings needed to be changed once or twice daily for the first few days. I wasn't allowed to get them wet. I was scheduled to see Dr. W in a couple weeks so that she could examine the incisions and monitor how I was healing.

When I went to the post-op visit, Dr. W was very pleased with how my incisions looked. I can honestly say that she did the best job on my breast. I have a small scar that is about an inch long and is very close to the areola. She did this so that if I wear a bikini or a low-cut shirt (not that I do), my scar will not be visible. She emphasized that from now on I could only use my right arm to have blood drawn and my blood pressure taken. This was because she had removed lymph nodes from my left side. If a tourniquet is used on my left arm, because I have fewer lymph nodes, there is a chance I could develop lymphedema. Lymphedema is swelling and often discoloration of an affected limb (in my case it would be my arm). It can cause pain and infection. So, I always make sure that it is only my right arm used for having blood drawn and my blood pressure taken, and thankfully, I have never experienced lymphedema. Dr. W claimed that her part of my treatment was over, but that I needed to follow up with an oncologist. She recommended a woman named Dr. R and gave me all of her contact information. Dr. W had taken such good care of me that I was sorry not to have to see her again, yet glad because that meant I no longer needed a breast surgeon.

I scheduled an appointment with Dr. R in early January at a time when both my husband and I could attend. We sat in the waiting room for a fairly long time before we were ushered into an exam room. We seemed to wait there a long time too, but it was well worth it! Dr. R entered with a ream of printer paper that was accordion folded and had perforated tear off strips at each end and between each sheet. She proceeded to explain all about how cancer grows in the breast – talking, writing notes on the paper, and even drawing diagrams. My diagnosis was stage one invasive breast cancer. All breast cancers start in the milk ducts. If it stays there, it is called DCIS which stands for ductal carcinoma in situ. If it breaks out of the ducts into surrounding tissue, it is called invasive. That is what mine had done because it was no longer in the ducts. It had appeared to be only about eight millimeters on the ultrasound, but Dr. R clarified that when it was removed, it was measured to be one centimeter. That put me in an interesting situation. The treatment used to be lumpectomy with radiation for any tumors under one centimeter and the addition of chemotherapy for malignancies over one centimeter. Mine was exactly one centimeter, so should I be treated with chemotherapy? Dr. R suggested that my tumor be tested with OncoDX. She informed us that the only lab in the country that would do this particular test was in California. OncoDX would break down the cells to the DNA level to determine if there was any benefit to having chemotherapy. It was a very expensive test, so she would have to contact my insurance company to make sure they would cover it, and then she would let us know. If I was going to have chemotherapy, it would be done before the radiation, so for now I would have to wait. Dr. R also disclosed that my tumor was tested to see if it was estrogen receptive and HER-2 positive (human epidermal growth receptor 2). Mine was estrogen receptive but not HER-2 positive. By being estrogen receptive, it meant that the tumor used estrogen in my body to grow. After radiation, I would need to be on a specific medication for five years to fool my body into thinking I did not have any estrogen in the hopes of not having any new growths. Had it been HER-2 positive, I would have needed treatment with other drugs also. Dr. R supplied us with a wealth of information and patiently answered every single one of our questions. It was the longest doctor's appointment I ever had. I'm sure we were with her for over an hour. As we gathered all of the papers she had written on and stood to leave, she came over and gave me a hug. To this day, at every single appointment I have with her, she ends it with a hug. She is the most caring, sensitive, genuine, and compassionate doctor (and person) I have ever met!

After a week or so, I got a call from Dr. R's office confirming that my insurance company would cover the test. A piece of my tumor was going to be sent from the surgi-center to the lab in California, and Dr. R would meet with me again when she received the results. In the meantime, she suggested I consider being tested to see if I have the mutation of the BRCA gene, the hereditary breast cancer gene. It's a simple blood test. I decided it was important to know since I have two sisters and two daughters. I was tested, and fortunately, I do not have the mutation.

When I went back to meet with Dr. R to find out the results of the OncoDX test, she again described my situation as interesting. The test labels tumors into three categories. The first category is a non-aggressive cancer where chemotherapy would have little benefit. The third category is an aggressive cancer where chemotherapy is definitely recommended. Mine fell into the middle category where it's a somewhat aggressive cancer and there is some benefit to having chemo. Dr. R explained that all studies of cancer treatments check recurrence rates after ten years. She informed me that based on my OncoDX results, if I just had radiation, I would have a ninety-one percent chance of no recurrence in ten years, but if I had chemo, I would have a ninety-five percent chance of no recurrence after ten years. A four percent benefit! Was it worth it to go through all of the side effects of chemotherapy for a four percent improvement? Chemotherapy was scary to me. I've only heard horror stories about how debilitating the side effects are, especially the nausea. I hate to throw up and that was my biggest fear! She explained that if I decided to have the chemo, she would use two different drugs: Adriamycin and Cytoxan. I would be given them once every other week for a total of eight weeks. In other words, I would have four cycles of the medicine spread out over eight weeks. After hearing her description, I concluded that I needed time to think it over. I informed her that I would get back to her soon.

Meanwhile, I went home and researched the side effects of both drugs. Most common were nausea, vomiting, diarrhea, and hair loss. This was a difficult decision. I was trying to rate the pros and cons. My father, who is a retired internist, suggested I get a second opinion. He said, "Since you live close to

Johns Hopkins in Baltimore, why don't you consider trying to get a second opinion there?" What a fabulous idea! That's exactly what I did.

I ended up seeing a female breast surgeon at Johns Hopkins who recommended, based on my age (I was forty-six), that I have chemotherapy. She commented that she was attending a meeting of several breast specialists the next day and that she would bring up my case at the meeting. She promised me that she would let me know what the other doctors decided afterwards. True to her word, she called me the next day and reported that it was unanimous. Every doctor agreed that based on my age, the cancer type, and the results of the OncoDX test, they would definitely recommend that I have chemo. Even before she called, I also had been thinking that I was probably going to go ahead with it. I realized I would be upset if I didn't and then ended up with a recurrence. You know what they say, "coulda, woulda, shoulda!" So I called Dr. R's office and let them know I wanted to have chemotherapy. Well, I didn't want to have it, but I agreed to have it!

It was now mid-January. My chemotherapy was scheduled to start on Monday, February 12, 2007. I had returned to work on January 2nd and had informed my principal that I would continue to teach while I was undergoing radiation, as long as I could handle it. Now that I had made the decision to have chemotherapy, I didn't want to work all day and then come home and be so spent that I had nothing left for my own kids. I decided it would be best to take sick leave for the rest of the school year. I met with my principal and explained that Friday, February 9th would be my last day of that year, but that I planned to be back in the fall. On the Monday before my last day, my principal called me into his office and announced that he needed to do what was best for the students. In my school district, the policy was that teachers could take up to sixty days leave and be guaranteed their position when they came back. If they took more than sixty days, they would be guaranteed a position in the county, but not necessarily the one that they had left. If they took more than sixty days, it was up to the principal to decide if he/she wanted to advertise the position or hold it for the teacher. From February 9th until the last day of school was seventy-two days, twelve over the limit. My principal indicated that he had decided to advertise my position! I was shocked! Not only was I dealing with a cancer diagnosis, but I was also dealing with the fear of a looming chemotherapy treatment, not knowing what to expect. Now I had the added stress of not having a job when I was ready to return to work! I don't remember what I said to him and left his office stunned.

That night when I shared the exchange with my husband, he helped me draft a letter to my principal. This principal had never seen me teach and really didn't know me. I don't remember the exact letter, but I remember the gist. I explained that as difficult as it was to go through a cancer diagnosis and treatment, it was even more difficult to go through it and not know if I had a job to return to, or if I did, where it would be located. I pointed out that I had been teaching in the county since 1984 and had always received glowing evaluations. I added that I had a master's degree in mathematics and was secondary certified to teach math which made me highly qualified to teach the Algebra and Geometry classes that I was teaching at his school. I placed the letter in an envelope and set it in my principal's mailbox the next morning. The rest of the week I spent teaching my classes and writing notes for the substitute who would cover for me for the rest of the year.

On Friday, I was reassuring my students that they would be in good hands with the substitute, and I was trying not to feel too apprehensive about the upcoming week. During my planning period, I walked to the office to check my mailbox, and the administrative secretary mentioned that she needed me to come into her office to fill out some forms. I went in and filled out forms that stated what kind of leave I was taking and the dates of my leave. Dr. R had already submitted the doctor's note for me to use the sick leave bank, but I had to fill out my part at school. Just as I had with my month leave for voice therapy after my thyroidectomy, I got paid leave. Each year teachers get ten sick days and three personal days. If a teacher donates one of his or her sick days to the sick leave bank each year, he or she is a member. After using up all of his or her leave, the next three days of leave are without pay. Then the sick leave bank reimbursement begins by paying for the rest of the leave and retroactively for the three days. As I was filling out the paperwork, the principal poked his head in and requested I stop by his office once I had completed the forms.

After handing the completed forms to the secretary, I entered the principal's office. He commented, "I read your letter and I agree with everything you said. I will not advertise your position and you have a job here next year." I was immensely relieved. I thanked him and could now begin my cancer treatment with one less thing to worry about.

The next night, my husband and I went to dinner at a restaurant with my sisters and their husbands. My sisters had arranged it. They wanted me to have an enjoyable dinner out (without having to cook) before my treatment began. I shared with them that I was very nervous and afraid that I was going to be frequently throwing up from the chemo. They tried, as best as they could, to reassure me that I would get through this soon enough – four treatments wasn't too bad we all agreed. However, it was easier for them to say because it wasn't happening to them, and for me, fear of the unknown is a horrible thing!

The rest of the weekend went by in a blur, as I was feeling apprehensive about what Monday would bring.

On Monday morning I woke up early and bade goodbye to Lani and Valerie as they left for the bus stop. I had received a prescription for a medication called Emend to prevent nausea during chemotherapy. The directions stated to take one pill an hour before each chemo treatment. The co-pay for the one pill was twenty-five dollars! That seemed expensive for just one pill, but if it prevented nausea, it was well worth it in my mind! My husband wanted to accompany me to the appointment. I swallowed the large pill at the T-1 hour timeframe, and waited until it was time for us to leave.

When we arrived at Dr. R's office, we were escorted into the room called the infusion room. It's filled with lots of comfy Barcalounger type chairs. The nurse directed me to sit in one of them. She explained that I would be getting two IVs before the chemo started. One was an anti-nausea medicine and the other was something like Zantac to coat my stomach. Then after I had finished receiving those, she would administer the two chemo drugs. Adriamycin has to be given carefully. It can cause serious damage to surrounding tissue if it escapes the vein. She explained that she would be injecting it with a syringe so that she could watch as it went in and to monitor that it was not leaking out of the vein. Then the Cytoxan would be put in the same IV as the two anti-nausea medications. The whole process would take about two to three hours.

I surveyed the room and noticed it was filled with people who appeared to be significantly older than I was. That seemed to drive the point home to go for the most aggressive treatment since I was so young at the time. There was a man who I guessed to be in his eighties. There was a woman with a hat covering her bald head, who appeared to be in her sixties. Observing her bald head, I asked the nurse about when I could expect to start losing my hair. Hair loss is a side effect of AC (the name doctors and nurses use when referring to the combination of Adriamycin and Cytoxan). She claimed that I would begin to notice hair loss in anywhere from ten to twelve days.

So, before I started my next round of AC, I would already be losing my hair!

When all of the Cytoxan, the last part of my chemo, had dripped out of the IV bag and into my arm, I asked the nurse what to expect when I got home. She provided me with some anti-nausea pills. She instructed me to take them every eight hours for that day and the next, and then as needed after that. She warned me to stay extra hydrated and to drink as much as possible. She recommended Gatorade in any flavor. I confided in her that I was nervous that the chemo was going to make me throw up. She replied, "You contact us if you are even the slightest bit nauseous. We want to deal with it right away. We don't want you to even feel nauseous so we don't expect you to throw up." I wanted to hug her. If they could prevent me from being nauseous, I wouldn't have to worry about throwing up.

The nurse and Dr. R then suggested I have a port inserted for the remaining three treatments. A port is small disc that is temporarily implanted under the skin. It can be made of plastic or metal. A catheter connects the port to a major vein. IV medications such as chemotherapy can be given directly into the port, and blood can be drawn from it ("How is Chemotherapy Given?"). With a port, the nurse wouldn't have to sit and slowly inject the Adriamycin with a syringe because it could be administered directly and safely into the port. I gave the okay and Dr. R arranged the appointment for that Friday.

My husband dropped me off at home before stopping at the grocery store to pick up my favorite flavor of Gatorade – grape. I drank most of the bottle, had lunch, and then shuffled upstairs to take a nap. I am not a "take naps" type of person, yet I slept for two hours! I didn't know then, but found out later that a common side effect of anti-nausea medication is drowsiness. That coupled with the chemo drugs working their magic in my body, and I was wiped out. Because of this, I actually ended up taking a two-hour nap every day while undergoing chemotherapy! I took the anti-nausea medication the first two days, and I am happy to report that I never felt nauseous then or for any future chemo infusions. I did, however, experience chemo brain.

Chemo brain started the next day. It is difficult to describe. It's an overall feeling of brain fog. Your thinking is slow and muddled. I also define it as the feeling you have when you are coming down with something or have a low grade fever. All day Tuesday and part of Wednesday, I suffered from it. I didn't feel terrible, but I didn't feel well either.

On Friday, I trekked to the hospital next to Dr. R's office, and a very young doctor explained what he was going to do. He was going to give me light sedation (I would still be awake) and then insert the port in my right arm. Since it was my left breast, he chose the right arm. I'm not sure why he selected my arm, since most people have ports inserted in their chest just under the collarbone, and I didn't think to ask him. I remember chatting with the nurse before the procedure. She was asking me how I felt and I muttered that I had received the chemo on Monday and had gotten my period on Tuesday. "Just add insult to injury!!!" I said. She informed me that chemo causes many women to stop menstruating. I replied, "At least there's one good thing about having chemo," and we both laughed. Sure enough, it was the last period I ever had!

During the surgery, I didn't feel any pain. I remember feeling a lot of pressure as if the doctor kept trying to push something between my skin and my bones in my arm. I guess that's exactly what he did! The port was actually two discs, like a figure eight, inside the middle of my upper right arm. The whole surgery took approximately fifteen minutes.

The next part of my treatment was to return to Dr. R's office the following Monday to have my blood drawn. One of the side effects of chemotherapy is a drop in red and white blood cells. On the Mondays that I wasn't having chemo, I was scheduled to have my blood tested. If my levels were low, I would receive a shot of something to signal my bone marrow to produce more blood cells. The first Monday blood check came back with positive results. My counts were normal, and I didn't need anything.

Having the blood drawn from the port was an interesting experience. First, the skin covering the port was swabbed with an antiseptic wipe (just like any time blood is drawn, even without a port). Then a needle was inserted into one of the discs. As soon as the needle went in, it was as if I could taste the antiseptic wipe. I immediately tasted what rubbing alcohol smells like. The nurse claimed that this sensation was common. In fact, there were lemon drops kept in the infusion room for patients to suck on at the start of chemo in the hopes that the lemon taste would mask the rubbing alcohol taste and be more pleasant.

Dr. R had written a prescription for a wig. I think she had called it a hair prosthetic! Ha! By writing it that way, I could purchase a wig and my insurance would cover the cost of it. I discovered a place that sold wigs called Amy of Denmark. It was not far from my house. Amy's was known to be great for cancer patients. I asked Betsy and another friend (I can't remember who it was) to join me. Amy's had a huge selection. My hair is naturally dark brown with a considerable amount of wave and curl. I had been wearing it between chin and shoulder length in the back and in shorter layers near my face. I decided to take the depressing situation of being a cancer patient who would soon lose all of her hair and make it fun. I tried on some crazy wigs. I was able to see myself with long blond hair, a big afro, and many wacky styles and colors. We stayed there for a few hours laughing the whole time! In the end, I settled for something very close to my natural color and current style.

The rest of that week was relatively uneventful. On Sunday, though, I noticed a change. I was sitting on the couch reading a book, and I ran my fingers through my hair. I saw that I had two strands of hair on my hand. I tried it a few more times, and each time my hand came away with two more strands of hair. It had been thirteen days since I had started chemo. My hair loss was right on schedule. By

Monday morning, my hand came away with four or more strands of hair on it.

On the Monday of my second round of chemo, I assured my husband that he didn't need to accompany me, and he could stay home and get his work done. I have always been strong and independent. My parents always tease me because of something I announced when I was about six years old. I was trying to learn how to ride my two-wheel bike without training wheels. I would ride it down the driveway, fall, walk it up the driveway, and repeat the process. My parents offered to help me, but I refused. I shouted, "I'll do it myself!" I must have fallen at least twenty times, but eventually I got the hang of it and was proud that I had accomplished it all by myself. I've been that way ever since! In many ways, I prefer being by myself at doctors' appointments. If I'm uncomfortable, I don't have to put on a show for anyone and act like everything is all right. Some people really need other people to be there in situations like this, but I am perfectly at ease going by myself. I gulped down my Emend and drove to Dr. R's office.

This time, all happened as the first time, except there was no syringe of Adriamycin. As the nurse started the IV, I opted to suck on a lemon drop to avoid the antiseptic taste (which I still did taste a little even with the lemon drop). First, there was the bag of one anti-nausea medicine. When it was empty, it was followed with the second bag of anti-nausea medicine. After the second bag had completely dripped into me, it was replaced with a bag of

Adriamycin. When that bag was empty, it was exchanged for the Cytoxan. I was conversing with the nurse and showed her how I was starting to lose my hair. She was not surprised. She asked if I had a wig. I replied that I had one, but that I had also purchased special hats. They looked like baseball caps but came down lower over the ears. They were made of cotton so they were extremely soft. I bought four of them: red, pink, black, and denim. I planned to wear whichever color matched my clothes. She commented, "What a great idea! I look forward to seeing you in a hat next time." She recommended that I purchase a special sleeping cap. She informed me that many cancer patients are surprised by how cold they are at night because they never realized how much their hair kept their heads warm. I told her that I would order one from the same website that I had purchased the other hats. It's a great website with all kinds of cancer products: www.headcovers.com.

On Tuesday morning (the next day), after Lani and Valerie left for school, I turned to my husband and announced that I wanted him to shave my head. I knew my hair was going to fall out, and I figured it would be less traumatic if I shaved my head than to wake up with clumps of hair on my pillow one morning or to watch those clumps go down the drain in the shower. He was surprised, but thought that it was a fantastic idea. We moseyed up to the bathroom, and he extracted his electric razor from the back of the cabinet under the sink. He used that razor sporadically to trim his sideburns and mustache. We decided to have a little fun. He shaved my head in parts, and we took pictures. I sported a Mohawk in one. In another, I had short hair on one side and long hair on the other. One of us would describe a wacky look, and he proceeded to make it happen. We spent about two hours shaving my head and laughing the whole time. I have more pictures of me with very unusual hairstyles than I can count! Afterwards, I donned the denim hat to go with my outfit of jeans and a sweater. When Lani and Valerie came home from school, my husband greeted them at the door and warned them about what we had done. Then I sauntered around the corner. They both smiled and said I looked great! I love my daughters!

I don't know if it was the emotional strain of shaving my head, the fact that I had just had my second round of chemo, or if it was a combination of the two, but I was feeling rather sick. I wasn't nauseous and I don't know exactly how to describe it. I just felt awful. I also had the fuzzy feeling in my head of chemo brain. After the first round, I had felt better by Wednesday. This time the sick and foggy feeling lasted through Thursday. Ugh!

On Friday, I put on one of my hats to match the outfit I was wearing that day, and headed to the grocery store. At home, I tended to wear nothing on my head and walked around bald. I was a little too self-conscious to do that out of the house. So, donning my hat, I left to pick up some groceries. After paying the cashier, I started pushing my cart full of groceries toward the exit. I passed a bench where an elderly woman was sitting. She looked at me in my hat and declared, "It's going to be all right, dear." At first I was upset. I thought, "She doesn't know anything about my situation. I could have been informed that I have only months to live." (Thankfully, I've never been told that). I wanted to make a snarky retort in response, but then I thought about what I had learned after my husband made the comment about my breast cancer that I had thought was so insensitive. I remembered that most people want to be kind and don't always know what to say. She was probably just trying to be positive and encouraging. So, I just thanked her and continued on my way.

Another interesting interaction I had was at the gym. I wouldn't call myself a gym rat, but I try to go three to four times a week to do both aerobic and weight-bearing exercises. Unfortunately, now that I had a port, I was only permitted to do light exercise such as walking. I was not allowed to do anything with weights. I desperately wanted to walk, and it was too cold to walk outside, so I decided to go to the gym on days that I felt well enough. I thought it would help my healing process to walk for about an hour. I didn't go on infusion days, but I tried to go every other day. I noticed that my cotton hats made me feel quite sweaty even though I was walking at a leisurely pace. I ended up buying several bandanas that were lighter weight. I could tie them around my head in a way to cover up my baldness but not make me feel like I was cooking underneath. At that time, the gym I belonged to had imposed a thirty minute time limit on the treadmills. I guess some clients were on them for a very long time, and other clients were upset because they had to wait for one to become vacant. One morning, I had been walking for about forty minutes when a gym employee approached me and said that I was over my time limit and needed to get off. I am usually the type of person who avoids confrontation and is a stickler for obeying rules, but I was paying for a membership to the gym, and this was the only exercise I was allowed to do. I didn't want to get off. I calmly asserted myself and informed the employee, "I'm currently undergoing chemo and this is the only exercise I am permitted to do." He looked so contrite and told me by all means to continue for as long as I wanted.

That weekend, my husband and I had dinner plans with another couple at a restaurant. I decided that because we were going to a restaurant, it would look nicer if I wore my wig rather than one of my hats. My wig looked good on me, almost natural, but it wasn't totally comfortable. It came with a thin cotton head cover to put on between the wig and my scalp, but even with that, the wig was a little itchy. I think I have very sensitive skin! Or maybe I was just imagining it because I was self-conscious and thought everyone could tell it was a wig, even though those who knew told me it looked very natural. They admitted that they wouldn't be able to tell if they didn't know, but I still felt self-conscious. I resolved to stick it out for one dinner, but just in case, I brought along one of my hats to change into if I got too uncomfortable. We ended up having a delightful dinner, and I forgot all about the wig. As we exited the restaurant, I noticed it had started to rain. Instinctively, I started to pull my jacket up over my head, but then I realized I wasn't feeling any rain! My wig was covering my head and protecting my scalp. It was one of the strangest sensations!

That Monday, I returned to Dr. R's office for my blood count check. Unfortunately, one of my counts was lower than it should have been. The nurse informed me that I would need a shot of something that would direct my bone marrow to kick into high gear and produce more of that blood cell. The nurse warned me that the shot is more painful than most. She confided that many people prefer to be injected in their stomach rather than in their arm because the muscle there is thicker and it doesn't hurt as much. I had never gotten a shot in my belly before so I decided to try it. She wasn't kidding. It was quite painful!

That evening after dinner, I was sitting on the couch watching TV. I started to feel achy in my back like I had been sitting in a bad position. I mentioned it to my husband, and he offered to give me a back rub. I thought that was sweet of him and that it would probably feel great. Boy was I wrong! The second he put his hands on my back and put even the slightest amount of pressure, I screamed and jumped up. I cannot even begin to describe how excruciating it was. I could not stand to have anything touch my back! He was stunned, too. I had never acted that way before.

I was fairly uncomfortable for the rest of the night, but fortunately it didn't prevent me from getting a decent night's sleep. I woke up in the morning and felt the pain had lessened. I called Dr. R's office to tell them about what happened. It turns out that the pain meant that the shot had been effective. What I had been feeling was the bone marrow working in my back to produce more blood cells.

The following Monday, I was set to have infusion number three. I had read about a special cream that I could rub on the skin of my arm over the port to help numb the pain of the IV. I had to apply it about an hour before the appointment and then cover the area with Saran wrap until I got to the infusion room. It felt and looked unusual, but it was great! It really did numb the pain. I didn't feel the needle at all!

Infusion number three transpired the same as the previous one. I did mention to the nurse that I had felt rather sick after the second one. She reproached me for not calling the office and relaying that to them because they didn't want me to be uncomfortable at all. I'm not a complainer and I thought that how I had been feeling was to be expected with chemo. She claimed that a lot of people don't feel well because they get dehydrated even if they are not vomiting. She suggested that I come in on Tuesday to receive IV fluids. She promised that it would help me feel less sick. She also informed me that most people describe the second round as the worst of the four. I thought that was interesting and hoped it was the case because then this round and the next one would be easier.

On Tuesday, I headed back to Dr. R's office, and a big bag of IV fluid was injected through my port. It took about an hour. Sure enough, the nurse was right. I didn't feel as terrible. I still had chemo brain and a dull sick feeling until Friday, but it wasn't as bad as the second round.

The next week, my blood was tested, and I prayed that my counts would be normal. I didn't want to experience that painful shot to boost my blood count again or the even more intense agony of the shot working. Luckily, my counts were normal. No shot! Yay! As it turned out, I never needed another one after that.

I couldn't believe it. I was almost done. One more round of chemo and I would have completed that phase of my treatment. Dr. R had warned me that she would closely monitor my temperature because I could not have chemo if I had a fever. If I did run a fever, I would probably need to be hospitalized because my immune system was compromised due to the chemo. Well, on Wednesday of the week before my last chemo, both my husband and Valerie came down with a virus that consisted of a high fever and a cough. I banished my husband to the guest room to sleep, and I stayed in my bedroom. When I left the bedroom to go to the kitchen to get something to eat, I armed myself with a can of Lysol and sprayed the air ahead of me as I walked, the banister on the stairs before I touched it, and the kitchen cabinet knobs before I touched them. Basically, I emptied almost the entire can of Lysol in two days! I washed my hands constantly also. By Friday, both of their fevers had broken, and I came out of seclusion in my bedroom. Miraculously, even though my immune system was compromised, I never contracted the virus. I was able to receive my last round of chemo on time. No delay!

The last round seemed to be the same as the third one. I returned the next day for IV fluids since that had helped so much before. I was incredibly happy to be done, but the dull sick feeling and chemo brain lingered for a very long time. I don't think I started to feel like myself until at least two weeks later.

I am so grateful that I made it through all four rounds of chemo without ever being nauseous. The combination of Emend, the two IV anti-nausea drugs, and the anti-nausea pills really worked!

Dr. R explained that I would get a break before I started radiation but recommended that I meet with the radiation oncologist, Dr. A, to get everything all arranged. The radiation oncologist's office was around the corner from Dr. R's office. I was glad it was so conveniently close because the standard course of radiation is every day, Monday through Friday, for six and a half weeks! I met with Dr. A, who explained the whole process to me. Afterwards, he instructed me to lie down on a table while he aligned the radiation machine to direct the radiation exactly where it needed to be. Dr. A didn't start the machine. I didn't receive any radiation yet. He was just getting everything set up. As I was lying on the table, he used something that looked like Sharpie to tattoo my body in several places. These would be guiding marks so that each time I had radiation, everything would be aligned exactly the same. The marks were not permanent, but did not wash off easily either, and I had to make sure that I didn't scrub too hard and wash them off in the shower. To direct the beam of radiation to hit the exact spot in my breast, Dr. A made a mold of what looked and felt like a small piece of plaster. It would be placed on spots also labelled with tattoos on my breast. He explained that the mold helped direct the depth of the radiation beam to hit exactly where he needed. I was informed that each time I came, I would go to a dressing room and take off everything from the waist up. I would put on a gown they provided and wait in the waiting room until the nurse was ready for me in the radiation room. After entering the radiation room, I would disrobe and lie on the table. The nurse would position me so that all of my tattoos were lined up as they were supposed to be, would put the mold on my breast, and then would start the machine. It would circle around my body and take less than five minutes. After that, I would be able to put on the gown, go back to the dressing room to get dressed, and then leave. Dr. A warned me that the radiation might cause my skin to look red and feel sunburned in the area being radiated. He suggested that I wear loose fitting clothes on top to be the most comfortable. Radiation was scheduled to start in mid-April, about three to four weeks after my last round of chemo.

The evening of the day I had met with Dr. A, I was describing to my friend Betsy what was going to be happening. She made an excellent recommendation. She suggested that I purchase a few of the camisoles that are designed with a built-in bra. She thought that they would be much more comfortable to wear than an actual bra, especially since I wear bras with underwires. I loved that idea and went out the next day to buy several.

After having been through chemo, radiation was not nearly as difficult. It didn't make me feel sick or give me chemo brain, but it was not comfortable either. Plus, having to go every day for six and half weeks was taxing! I was glad that the whole appointment really only took about fifteen minutes from start to finish, and most of that was the time it took me to undress and get back dressed again! The uncomfortable part was that I have fairly sensitive skin. I am very light skinned, and if I'm not careful, I will get a sunburn before I get a tan. The radiation was making the skin on my breast look very red. Dr. A prescribed a cream that I was allowed to use on my breast because it wouldn't reduce the effectiveness of the radiation and would lessen the irritation. It helped a little, but my breast was itchy, red, and raw. The worst part was that the skin on my nipple actually peeled off! To this day, my left nipple is a lighter color than my right one. I also have a permanent tan in the shape of the mold on my left breast. The radiation through the mold tinted my skin. I can say that the camisoles were very comfortable though. Thanks again, Betsy!

On June 6, 2007, I completed my last radiation treatment. When I stood up from the table, the nurse asked me to meet her in the exam room after I got dressed. When I entered the exam room, the entire staff of the radiation center was there. They presented me with a gift bag and a diploma! I was so surprised. I looked at the diploma and burst out laughing. It said that I had successfully completed my course of radiation! The gift bag was filled with all sorts of goodies. It had been donated by a volunteer group who did fundraising to help cancer patients. I don't remember everything it contained, but there was a stuffed animal wearing a note about hope, a book, a pen, and a few other items. I was extremely touched. I did it! I finished all of my treatment for breast cancer.

Dr. R informed me that for the first five years I would see her every three months for follow-up appointments. After that, I would graduate to every six months. She would draw blood at every visit to monitor my thyroid levels and make sure that my Synthroid dose was correct. The bloodwork would also check tumor markers for breast and thyroid cancer to make sure that those numbers were not elevated. In addition to the bloodwork, Dr. R would also perform a breast exam. I would need to alternate every six months between mammograms and breast MRIs for the first few years. After that I would revert to yearly mammograms, but they would always be diagnostic for the rest of my life. That would mean four views of each breast (instead of the usual two) would be taken each time. Every few years I would need a PET scan to make sure that all of my organs were cancer free. Dr. R prescribed a medication called Tamoxifen to fool my body into thinking that I didn't have any estrogen. That way, my body couldn't use estrogen to make another tumor. I would continue to take it for five years. All of this sounded like a good plan to me.

My experience with estrogen suppressive medication was interesting. I was on Tamoxifen for about two years. It is an effective drug for pre-menopausal women. I had not had a period since starting chemotherapy. Dr. R performed a blood test to verify that I was truly post-menopausal, and it confirmed that I was. Because of this, I had to switch to a different drug called Femara. Femara worked the same way as Tamoxifen but was effective in women who had already been through menopause. I needed to continue the Femara for a total of five years. So, because I had been on Tamoxifen for two years prior, I took estrogen suppressive medication for a total of seven years! The side effects of Femara consist of all of the typical menopause symptoms, the most common being hot flashes. Wow! No kidding! I used to always be cold. Now, you could fry an egg on me several times a day! The other most common side effect is joint pain. I didn't mind the hot flashes too much. They were annoying but kind of laughable. The joint pain was something else. I would wake up in the morning and hobble to the bathroom. It was as if I had arthritis. I had to stumble around for a little bit, and that seemed to get the kinks out. I noticed the same thing happening if I sat for a long time. As soon as I got up, I was stiff and sore. I tended to get aches in my knees several times a day. When I mentioned this to Dr. R, she informed me that I could take a vacation from the medication. That meant I would stop taking it for a month and then start up again. During the month, the side effects would go away, but once I resumed the medication, they would return. She said that if I could stick it out for about twelve to eighteen months, the side effects would probably disappear. I decided I would try to ride it out. I have attacked all of my cancers with the attitude that I will do whatever I have to do to treat them. In this case, if I took a break and then had a recurrence, I would be angry with myself and regret taking that break. I would have to carry on and fight through the discomfort. Dr. R was right. After about eighteen months, or possibly even a little less, I noticed I wasn't having any achiness or stiffness. I still have hot flashes to this day, even though I have not taken the Femara since 2014, but they are a lot less frequent and a lot less intense.

Cancer #3 Recurrence of Thyroid Cancer

I had finished my breast cancer treatment in June of 2007 and had gone back to teaching that fall. I didn't return to the school I had left. Even though my principal had redeemed himself by letting me know I still had a job when I came back from sick leave, the fact that he originally said I wouldn't had left me feeling like he was not the type of person I wanted as my supervisor. I decided to try to transfer to another school. There was an opening at one of the middle schools where I had hoped to work when I originally left elementary school. The principal of that middle school was holding interviews in April. It was while I was undergoing radiation treatment, but the interview was scheduled in the afternoon, and my treatment was in the morning. I donned a professional looking outfit and my wig, and then went into the bathroom to apply some make-up. I don't usually wear much, just some blush, eye-liner, and occasionally some mascara. When I went to apply the mascara, I was shocked to see that I only had about one-third of my eyelashes. I didn't know that the chemo had caused me to lose my eyelashes!

Even though I was self-conscious about my wig and was sure everyone could tell I was wearing one, the interview with the principal and two teachers from the school went well. I assured them that I would be returning from leave to start the next school year. Just before I left, I asked the principal when she would be making a decision. She replied that she had a few more candidates to interview and that it wouldn't be for a couple of days. I said, "I'm sure it is a difficult decision. I don't envy you in having to make that decision, but I hope that the decision is me!" Two days later, at 7:30 in the morning, she phoned and offered me the position. She emphasized that she was calling early before anyone else could offer me a position. That made me feel incredible! I thanked her, accepted, and didn't tell her that I hadn't interviewed anywhere else. I then wrote a letter to the former principal thanking him for everything. I didn't want to burn any bridges by transferring to a new school and never letting my former principal know. I explained that I accepted this position because it was closer to home. That was only a partial truth, but sometimes you can't be totally honest.

I was proud to be able to start the school year with my own hair. It had grown back remarkably curly, almost like an afro, and with much more white. It was so short, maybe an inch or two, that it was easy to manage. I thought I would feel uncomfortable and self-conscious teaching in a wig, and I didn't think my hats were appropriate at school, so I didn't cover my head and let everyone see my new hairdo. My hair continued to grow all year, and by the end of the school year, it looked exactly like it had before I started chemo, except for the additional white.

At the beginning of May, about six weeks before the end of the school year, I visited Dr. R for one of my follow-up visits. She performed all of the usual bloodwork. She checked my thyroid function to make sure my Synthroid dose was correct. This included checking the levels of T4 and TSH. T4 is the hormone produced by the thyroid. The pituitary gland produces TSH (thyroid stimulating hormone) to let the thyroid know how much T4 to secrete. If there is a lot of T4, the TSH level will be low to alert the thyroid that it does not need to secrete more T4. Conversely, if there is not a lot of T4, the TSH level will rise as the pituitary gland is signaling the thyroid to produce more of it. Dr. R also checked the tumor marker, thyroglobulin, to verify that no thyroid cancer cells were growing back. Thyroglobulin is a protein produced in normal thyroid cells. In a person with a thyroid, the level should be above thirty-five. After a thyroidectomy, the levels should drop. Prolonged treatment with Synthroid should cause the levels to fall below one. Dr. R. reported that while my T4 and TSH levels were normal, she didn't like that my thyroglobulin level was elevated. It was up to four! Previously, and for many years, it had been below one. She thought it might be lab error that caused the elevation and requested I come back for a repeat test. That one came back at seven! She believed that Dr. D had not been keeping me on a high enough dose of Synthroid to suppress growth and was concerned that some thyroid cancer cells had grown back. So was I! "Here we go again," I thought.

Dr. R instructed me to stop taking Synthroid for a few weeks in order to check my thyroid functions again, and she wanted me to have another radioactive iodine test like the one I had back in 1993. I took leave for the last two weeks of school because being off of Synthroid made me hypothyroid. The symptoms of hypothyroidism are lethargy and sluggishness, weight gain, and increased sensitivity to cold. I was definitely tired and spent all day on my screened-in porch where it was nice and warm during the month of June. Even though I felt so lethargic, it was nice to veg out on the porch and to not have to think about work. Unfortunately, the radioactive iodine test revealed cells where my thyroid used to be. That proved that some thyroid cancer cells had indeed grown back.

Dr. R prescribed a treatment called I-131 which is a much higher dose of radioactive iodine than the test. The test had just enough radiation to make the cells visible. I-131 had enough radiation to kill the cells. First, I would have to eat a low iodine diet for three weeks prior to the treatment. This would help attract the radioactive iodine to the thyroid cells. Then I would be hospitalized for three days. I would swallow two pills containing the radioactive iodine. Because of the high radiation levels, I would have to complete this in the hospital in a special room designed just for this procedure. No one would be able to come too close to me for fear of exposure to radiation. Special precautions had to be taken when I went to the bathroom because my urine and feces would contain radiation for several days after the treatment. After the three days, I would be permitted to return home.

The three week low-iodine diet was somewhat challenging. I had plenty of choices, but it was not easy to eat out. I was not allowed anything with salt since iodine is usually added to salt. Ordinarily, it wouldn't be too troublesome to avoid eating out for three weeks, but we had relatives visiting from Europe and had planned a vacation with them to show them a beautiful part of upstate New York. I did the best I could but couldn't wait to be off of that diet.

When I checked in to the hospital, I was guided to a room that had a radiation hazard sign on the door. It was a little disconcerting to know that I was going into that room! The sign warned that all visitors must check in with the desk first. When I walked in, I noticed strips of paper, like what is used to cover exam tables in doctors' offices, lining the floor between the bedroom and the bathroom. I was warned to only walk on the paper and to not step directly on the floor! So many precautions! I got myself settled and was chatting with my husband. He was going to stay until they gave me the pills. Not too long later, a doctor entered the room, and I was shocked at how he was dressed. He resembled an astronaut in a spacesuit or a person in a hazmat uniform! He was carrying a container that looked like it was from a sci-fi movie. It was a huge metal container that was sealed and had a huge radiation hazard sticker on it. With gloved hands, he unsealed the container and pulled out a plastic cup containing two capsules. I chuckled when I saw the cup because the container was at least ten times larger than it was! He instructed me to take the cup and put the pills in my mouth without touching them. He stressed that I was not allowed to touch them. I tipped the cup into my mouth and tossed the pills back. He then handed me a cup of water, and I swallowed both pills. That was it. It seemed sort of anti-climactic after all the safety precautions leading up to it!

I didn't really feel anything, and soon it was dinner time. My dinner tray arrived with a decent looking meal, well as decent as hospital food can be, and a plate with a whole lemon sliced up. The male nurse who brought in the tray explained that a common side effect of I-131 is reduction in saliva or clogged salivary glands. It was important that I suck on the lemon slices, which he said would be provided with every meal, to encourage my salivary glands to work. I don't mind lemons so that was okay with me. I-131 causes some people lose their sense of taste or have significant changes to it, and for some people this is permanent. Luckily, that didn't happen to me. I remember a metallic taste for the first few meals, but then it went away.

The three days passed rather uneventfully. I watched TV and read the books and magazines I had brought with me so I wasn't too bored. I kept to my paper path when I went to the bathroom, and I ate my meals with a course of lemons.

When I went home, there were precautions I had to take to prevent exposing others to radiation. First, I had to use a separate bathroom. I was not allowed to use the same one that the rest of my family used. Second, after every time I went to the bathroom, I had to flush the toilet at least three times. This had to continue for a while (I don't remember exactly how long, but it was at least three days). The rest of the summer (about two weeks) was no different from previous summers, and I enjoyed my time off before starting another school year. The only troubling thing I noticed was that I lost my voice after coming home from the hospital. At first I was worried that it was a repeat of what happened after my thyroidectomy and that I would need voice therapy again. Dr. R assured me that it was a common side effect of I-131 and not to worry. Sure enough, it only lasted about a week.

There was one precaution I was informed of but never had the chance to experience. I was given a card to carry with me for three months explaining that I had had I-131. Supposedly, I had enough residual radiation in me that I could have set off the radiation detectors in the airport! Unfortunately, I didn't have any travel plans in the near future. I didn't go to the airport until more than three months later. I don't know if I would have set off the detectors, but I would have liked to see it happen!

Life was back to normal, except in September I noticed that I was getting nosebleeds and that the inside of my nose always felt gross and crusty. I had never had a nosebleed before in my life. I had bumped my nose pretty hard in the past when I clumsily walked into the wood frame of an open casement window. It smarted enough to make my eyes water, but never caused a nosebleed. I was concerned that now I was getting nosebleeds for no apparent reason, so I made an appointment with an ear, nose, and throat (ENT or otolaryngologist) doctor. He informed me that this was not too uncommon since I had had radiation to my throat and neck area which is close to my nose. He directed me to use a neti-pot to rinse my nose twice a day and prescribed a cream to use inside my nose that would help alleviate the crusty feeling. After about two weeks of this regimen, I felt totally back to normal until several years later.

I'm not sure if it's related to the I-131, but I have had an issue with my right nostril. I started having nosebleeds again out of the blue sometime in 2013. One morning I woke up and thought my nose was running. I grabbed a tissue from my nightstand drawer and proceeded to wipe my nose with it. The tissue was full of blood! Another time, as I was riding the escalator downstairs in DSW where I was shopping for shoes, my nose felt like it was running. Again, it wasn't just running, it was bleeding! Both times it was the right nostril, and it started for no apparent reason. I went to my ENT and she cauterized it. That was not a fun experience! However, it seemed to solve the problem until about two years later. I began having random bloody noses again. It was cauterized a second time which was worse than the first time. The doctor was surprised at how much my nose was bleeding while doing the cauterizing! Recently I suffered another severe nosebleed. I hope I do not need a third cauterization. If so, I may see if there is something else that can be done.

Cancer #4 Bladder Cancer

2015 was quite an eventful year because I retired from the school system and separated from my husband. I had taught for thirty-one years, so I was fully vested to receive my pension. Actually, I was fully vested the year before, but Valerie graduated in May of 2015, so I decided to wait until she was done before I retired. I was ready for a change in careers. Because of my math background, I completed some coursework during my last year of teaching and became QuickBooks certified. I hoped to get a job as a bookkeeper for my next career. My official retirement date from teaching was July 1, 2015. On July 6th, I started a job as a bookkeeper for a small accounting firm with two CPAs. I have worked there ever since and absolutely love it! My boss, Howard, couldn't be nicer and is extremely patient with me as I learn all of the finer details of bookkeeping. The funny thing about my retirement is that my last day in the county was in July, and at the end of August, Valerie started teaching music in an elementary school in the same county. It was just one month after I left! She had graduated with a degree in music education. I remarked to people that it was out with the old and in with the new!

As for my marriage, it had been great at the beginning. My husband had been supportive during my cancers. That was not the issue. It is complicated though, the story of another memoir perhaps? I can say that I was unhappy and had been for a while. I had been through enough physical heartache with all of my cancer treatments that I didn't need any emotional heartache as well. I felt I deserved to be happy and wanted to be with someone who made me feel that way and didn't bring me down. Remember how I mentioned that I believe respect is the most important character trait a person can possess and demonstrate to others? Sadly, somehow along the way, we lost respect for one another. I knew that I couldn't stay in that relationship. In September of 2015, I moved out of our marital home and into an apartment about twenty minutes away and only ten minutes from my new job. At that time, my husband and I had three cats, two of whom are brothers. We did not want to separate them, so we decided that they would spend alternating six weeks with each of us. A friend of mine called it "catimony," like alimony, but for cats! As it turned out, one of the cats had difficulty adjusting to the transfer and became aggressive which is a sign of stress in cats. Surprisingly, this only happened at the house and not at my apartment. I think animals sense their owner's emotional state. I tend to be calm and even-keeled, while my husband tends to be anxious and short-tempered. I think the cat sensed that. So, after switching them back and forth a few times, my husband decided I could keep them, and he ended up getting a new cat of his own.

In 2016, I was missing all of the things I had loved about teaching. I missed interacting with students and seeing the lightbulb go on in their heads when they learned a new concept. I heard about a tutoring job called Home and Hospital and applied. It was with the county I had retired from and involved working one-on-one with students who were too sick to go to school due to anxiety, surgery, or other health issues. The goal of the Home and Hospital instructor was to keep students current in their classes so that when they returned to school, they wouldn't be behind their classmates. It sounded perfect for me! The Home and Hospital office was thrilled to have a retired teacher on board since they wouldn't have to train me in curriculum. I started working with students at the beginning of March.

At the end of May in 2016, I came home from tutoring a Home and Hospital student and went to the bathroom. I stood up to flush the toilet and was horrified. The toilet was full of blood! I immediately pressed toilet paper against myself to see where it was coming from, but the toilet paper was clean. I checked my underwear, and it was clean too! I hadn't had a period since 2007! How could I have gotten a period again? Then I thought that maybe the cats had put something in the toilet that I didn't notice before I used it. What that something could be, however, I had no idea. What could the cats have dropped in the toilet to turn the water bright red? I was just so surprised. I guess I didn't want to believe anything was wrong with me, so I conjured up something completely ludicrous and highly unlikely to explain the situation. Isn't that what everyone does when they're shocked and scared? Or is it just me? I tried not to panic and decided I would wait to see if it happened again.

After dinner and watching TV for a while, I needed to use the bathroom again. It was around ten o'clock. This time I looked carefully in the toilet before I used it. It was empty. After using it, I was afraid to look. To my horror, it was full of blood again. I had tried not to panic before, but now it was a little harder to stay calm. What could it be? I had no pain so I didn't think it was a kidney stone. I had had one of those years before, and it had been excruciating. I had had a urinary tract infection (UTI) once before, but it had caused a burning sensation, and I didn't have any burning now. In fact, if I hadn't seen the blood, I wouldn't have known anything was amiss. I felt absolutely fine! A woman I know had an untreated UTI that became a kidney infection and she had developed a high fever. I didn't feel feverish, but decided to take my temperature anyway. Not surprisingly, it was normal.

So, now what should I do? Should I go to the emergency room? If I did, I would probably be there for hours, and who would feed the cats in the morning? I decided to wait and call my doctor in the morning. In the meantime, I googled causes of blood in urine. There were three causes listed: UTI, kidney stone, and bladder cancer. I didn't think I had a UTI or a kidney stone because I had had those before, and this time felt completely different. I was convinced I had bladder cancer.

That night I had a somewhat restless sleep. I kept dreaming about blood gushing from weird places in my body and toilets overflowing! I even got up to use the bathroom once in the middle of the night which I almost never do. Afterwards, when I looked in the toilet there was no blood! Now what was going on?

In the morning I showered and got dressed. There was no more blood when I went to the bathroom, but I decided I should still call my doctor. The receptionist insisted I come in and informed me that although my doctor was completely booked all day, there was a vacancy with the physician's assistant around 10:30. Even though I was disappointed that I couldn't schedule an appointment with my doctor, I decided to go. I emailed Howard and explained to him that I had a doctor's appointment and would try to come in to the office later.

Although the physician's assistant was reassuring, she did not have the correct diagnosis. She asked me to provide a urine sample so that she could check for infection. As I had assumed, there was no infection. The laboratory technician did see microscopic traces of blood even though I couldn't see it anymore. The physician's assistant suspected it was a kidney stone in spite of the fact that I had no pain. She suggested I receive an ultrasound of the abdomen and gave me the name of a urologist to follow up with in the next week. I called Howard and let him know that I wouldn't be in because my doctor wanted me to have an ultrasound. He wished me luck and told me not to worry about missing work.

Later that night, the physician's assistant called me back with the results of the ultrasound. There were no kidney stones visible. I was not at all surprised. She said that it was possible that I had already passed them. I doubted that and still was convinced I had bladder cancer. Meanwhile, I was scheduled to see a urologist named Dr. S four days later.

After meeting with the urologist, three things stick out in my mind. First of all, Dr. S is a young Asian woman. I was a little surprised when she first walked in because she looked so young. In fact, she looked to be about twelve years old! She was, however, extremely friendly, thorough, and knowledgeable. She explained everything in detail the same way Dr. R had when I first met with her. Dr. S asked me several questions to get a brief history and then showed me the views on her computer from my ultrasound. I could definitely see that I didn't have a kidney stone because she pointed to where it would be and what it would look like, and I didn't observe anything like what she described. According to her, everything else appeared to be completely normal. I took her word for it because I couldn't tell if anything looked abnormal from the view on the screen. I'm not a doctor and have always felt that I have no idea what I'm seeing when viewing x-rays and other scans, even though it is my own body which I think I know well! The second thing that stuck out in my mind was that she asked me if I had consulted "Dr. Google" when I first noticed the blood in the toilet. I chuckled at her choice of "Dr. Google" and admitted that I had. Dr. S emphasized that even though "Dr. Google" mentioned bladder cancer, she wanted to put me at ease. She informed me that in medical school she had to memorize the over one hundred different causes of gross hematuria, the medical term for visible blood in urine. Dr. S clarified that even though a bacterial infection was ruled out by the urinalysis, gross hematuria could be caused by a viral infection or fungal infection and that there were many other causes that weren't infections. The third thing that stuck out was when she asked about the chemotherapy treatment I received when I had breast cancer. She inquired about the drugs that were used. When I told her Cytoxan, her response was, "Hmmmmm." I thought, "I don't like the sound of that." She explained that studies of Cytoxan have shown that it increases the risk of bladder cancer due to the way it is excreted by the body. Cytoxan passes through the kidneys and the bladder. Thinking back, I guess that is why the nurse at Dr. R's office had urged me to drink a lot of fluids during chemo. Drinking would help flush the chemicals through my body. Dr. S wanted to schedule a cystoscopy, which is a scope of the bladder, as soon as possible. It was Tuesday and the earliest appointment she had was Friday.

On Friday, May 27, 2016, the cystoscopy was performed. I was nervous because I had never had one before and didn't know what to expect. The whole process took about thirty minutes. First I was instructed to go to the bathroom and empty my bladder. Then I undressed from the waist down in the room with the cystoscope. I positioned myself on the table under the paper "blanket." I was trembling a little due to nerves! Once I was covered up, the nurse returned and asked me to put my feet in stirrups. Then she said what Joan Rivers described as the words a woman most hates to hear, "Slide down!" I felt as if I was about to fall off the table! The nurse squirted a cold numbing gel in my "private area." She explained that it needed some time to work and that Dr. S would come in shortly. A few minutes later, Dr. S entered wearing her hair in a ponytail. When I first met her, I had thought she looked to be about twelve years old. Now, with the ponytail, she looked to be about nine!

A cystoscopy is similar to an ultrasound. A probe (called a cystoscope) with lenses on it is inserted into the urethra and then continues to the bladder. Connected to the probe is a tube used to fill the bladder with fluid, usually saline. The fluid expands the bladder so that the walls are smooth which helps to provide the best view. As the probe is moved all around, images of the bladder are visible on a screen similar to a TV or computer screen.

Dr. S inserted the cystoscope. Even with the numbing gel, it was mildly painful for a split second at first. My father explained to me that there is a sphincter at the opening of the urethra, and the pinch is felt as the probe passes through it. Dr. S started to fill my bladder with fluid. I couldn't exactly feel it, but I did have a mild sensation of needing to go to the bathroom again, even though I had just gone. Turning my head to the side, I was able to watch the screen. Dr. S was describing what we were seeing as she moved the probe all around my bladder. A few times we noticed water droplets. The screen was filled with a beige color that had some reddish lines through it. She explained that I was seeing the bladder wall and blood vessels. Then I was alarmed to spot a hole. I asked what that was and she replied that it was the opening from the ureter which brings the urine from the kidney. She found both of them and assured me they looked normal. Phew! At first I had thought the hole was a problem. Everything was going along fine until I noticed something unusual. It looked like a bunch of cauliflower or sea coral. I questioned what that was, and she calmly replied, "It's a tumor." I gasped and asked if she was going to biopsy it. She responded that she wanted to finish looking all around my bladder and then we would discuss it. A few minutes later, she was finished looking and removed the cystoscope. Dr. S advised me to get dressed, empty my bladder again, and then meet her in her office to discuss what she found.

So, now I was a little numb thinking my worst fear had been confirmed, and I had cancer for the fourth time. I got dressed and went to the bathroom. It was a strange sensation to go to the bathroom because my urine was cold. The fluid that had been instilled into my bladder had been room temperature which is significantly colder than body temperature. I walked shakily down the hallway to her office. On her desk was a photograph divided into four sections. Two of them were views of the tumor, and the other two showed other areas of the bladder. Dr. S admitted that bladder tumors can only be biopsied by having them surgically removed. She reported that we wouldn't know for sure whether or not it was cancer until it was biopsied but that to her it looked malignant! Great! She guided me down the hall to the surgical scheduler to book the surgery as soon as possible. It was May 27th, the Friday before Memorial Day, and the surgery was arranged for Tuesday, June 1st. Yay! What a birthday present a day early since my birthday is June 2nd. I also needed a quick physical and bloodwork from my primary care physician before the surgery could be performed. Luckily, my doctor squeezed me in that afternoon.

My primary care physician, Dr. I, came into the exam room for my pre-op physical with such a look of concern, I almost started to cry. She realized I had just gotten the news that I probably had cancer again and was wondering how I was feeling. I assured her I was doing okay. I don't think the reality had set in yet, but I usually don't get upset right away anyway. I remember her describing to me what happened when the physician's assistant examined me. The physician's assistant had left my exam room and told me she would be right back. I didn't know it at the time, but then she had gone to find Dr. I to inform her of my symptoms. The physician's assistant explained to Dr. I that she had done the urinalysis and suggested I have an ultrasound. She wanted to ascertain if there was anything else Dr. I wanted since Dr. I knew me and my history. Dr. I exclaimed that as soon as she heard that I was the patient, she asked the physician's assistant to make sure I got a follow-up appointment with a urologist. She remarked that she is aware of how in tune I am with my body so that if I discover anything unusual, it needs to be followed up in detail because I have had cancer so many times. I'm very glad she knows me and suggested I see a urologist!

Once again, the hardest part in all this was having to tell my daughters. I remember Lani had been upset that I hadn't discussed the events preceding my breast cancer diagnosis with her sooner. Even though I wouldn't know whether the tumor was benign or malignant until after the surgery, I wanted to divulge what was happening now and not wait until after the biopsy. My daughters were older than they had been when my breast cancer had been discovered. I called each one separately. I didn't want to have to do it over the phone, but it was difficult to arrange a time to get us all together before Monday due to their work schedules and busy lives. I called Lani first. I reminded her that she had been upset that I hadn't told her sooner about my breast cancer, so I wanted to share some news with her even though I didn't have all of the information yet. I explained everything that Dr. S had discussed with me. She cried and responded that this was terrible news. I wanted to be strong for her. I tried very hard not to cry also. I concurred that it was awful to have cancer again, but Dr. S was an excellent doctor, I would get through this, and everything would be okay. After we hung up, I relayed the same information to Valerie. She also cried, and I tried to be strong for her as well.

On Monday, my parents came to stay with me so that they could drive me to the surgi-center for the procedure on Tuesday morning. It was performed in the same place as the cystoscopy. I was scheduled for a TURBT which stands for trans-urethral resection of a bladder tumor. I wouldn't have a scar because like the cystoscopy, the tool for removing the tumor would be inserted into my urethra. I would be injected with a dye while under anesthesia (thankfully not a painful experience like the dye for the lymph node test when I had breast cancer) to ensure there were no tumors in the ureters or kidneys. The whole procedure would only take about thirty minutes.

The pre-op seemed to be the same as all of my prior surgeries except for one thing. When I settled myself on the table in the operating room, the nurse informed me that she would be positioning my legs in stirrups. She did, but then she wrapped a Velcro strap around them to keep them in place! I had the familiar feeling that my butt was hanging off the table. I never had surgery while in that position before! All surgical suites are kept at what I would describe as a freezing cold temperature. I think it's to keep the instruments working properly. So here I was, lying on the table with my privates exposed and feeling a wafting cold breeze on them. Before I could feel too uncomfortable though, the anesthesiologist administered the anesthesia, and I was out.

When I woke up from the anesthesia, Dr. S was standing next to my bed. She explained that bladder cancer is classified two different ways. One way to classify it is by the stage. All bladder cancers form in the bladder wall or lining. If the cancer remains only in the bladder lining, that is stage zero. If the cancer grows into the muscle layer or invades surrounding tissues and organs, it is stage one or higher. The other way to classify bladder cancer is by the grade. There is low grade which is not an aggressive cancer, or high grade which is. Dr. S believed that mine was low grade, but she wouldn't know for sure until the biopsy results came back. She then described a treatment using Mitomycin-C. Mitomycin-C is a chemotherapy drug that is an effective treatment for low grade bladder cancer. It must be instilled within twenty-four hours of a TURBT to obtain the best result. The problem was, Dr. S wouldn't receive the results of the biopsy for approximately a week. If she waited to give me the Mitomycin-C until after the biopsy report confirmed whether my cancer was low or high grade, it would be too late to be effective. Also, if my cancer turned out to be high grade, the Mitomycin-C would not have any benefit. After explaining all of this to me, Dr. S asked me if I wanted to go ahead with it. I could have her instill it now or I could come back tomorrow. Or, I could elect not to have it at all. The choice was mine. I decided that just like with opting to do chemotherapy for only a four percent better outcome when I had breast cancer, I was going to fight this cancer too. I didn't want to wait until tomorrow, however, because tomorrow was my birthday. I exclaimed, "Let's do it now!"

It was a bit embarrassing. After every surgery I've had, I always develop what I call "the trembles." I begin shaking uncontrollably all over my body for about an hour. It's similar to shivering from cold even though I'm warm. I think it's my body's reaction to anesthesia. Anyway, I was lying there trembling while Dr. S instilled the Mitomycin-C.

I then received all of my discharge instructions. I was scheduled to see Dr. S for a follow-up appointment on June 10th to find out the results of my biopsy. She forewarned me that she would not discuss the results over the phone. Great! More waiting for test results! My favorite activity! I was prescribed Uribel which is a pill to take for the burning I would feel in my bladder and sense of urgency to go to the bathroom once the pain medication that had been put in my IV during the TURBT wore off.

I took the Uribel right away when I got back to my apartment, but I was extremely uncomfortable. Pain from the surgery was understandable, but I think the Mitomycin-C exacerbated it. Going to the bathroom was so excruciating that the best way to describe it is that it felt like I was peeing shards of glass! Even with the medicine, I had to brace myself by holding onto the sides of the toilet when I had to go. I had to grit my teeth to prevent myself from crying out in agony! I was miserable feeling like I had to go to the bathroom constantly, but then equally as miserable when I went. It was like a catch-22. I didn't know which was worse – holding it in and having the sensation that I had to go, or just going and feeling the pain. Luckily, after the first twenty-four hours, with a combination of medication and time, the pain and urgency had lessened considerably. I was still uncomfortable, but not nearly as much as I had been at first. I was able to go out to dinner on my birthday with my parents, sisters, brothers-in-law, and daughters, and actually enjoyed it.

On June 10th, Dr. S confirmed that I did indeed have bladder cancer. The biopsy reported that it was high grade (so the Mitomycin-C was useless, but I don't regret having it). She informed me that it had not progressed to the muscle layer, which was a plus, but she wanted to do a further biopsy to be certain. Dr. S explained that the tumor was about three centimeters in size. She had taken samples of muscle tissue from one area, but she wanted specimens from the entire section of the lining that encompassed the tumor to make sure there were no cancer cells in the muscle layer somewhere else. High grade cancers are more aggressive, have a greater chance of recurrence, and are treated differently from low grade cancers. Muscle invasive bladder cancer is not managed the same way as non-muscle invasive cancer. We had to know exactly what we were dealing with to treat it effectively. High grade bladder cancer has an eighty percent recurrence rate. Unfortunately, if it recurs, it often progresses to the muscle layer or beyond. Since mine was high grade, Dr. S needed to get an exact diagnosis and treat it aggressively to prevent a recurrence. Therefore, I was scheduled for another TURBT on June 27th.

The results of the biopsy on June 27th were both good and bad. The good news was that there truly was no cancer in the muscle layer and it was limited to the bladder lining. The bad news was that a second aggressive cancer was discovered near the site of the tumor that had been removed. There are two main types of bladder tumors. One type is a papillary carcinoma. It grows up from the lining into the hollow area of the bladder, kind of like a mushroom. That is the tumor that we had seen on the cystoscopy and that Dr. S had extracted. The second type is flat and is called carcinoma in situ (CIS). It stays low on the lining of the bladder like a carpet. It is an aggressive cancer. So, in essence, I had both a high grade papillary tumor and high grade CIS!

Dr. S spent a long time discussing my treatment plan. She insisted I have a chest x-ray, and both an MRI and CT scan of the abdomen and pelvis. Bladder cancer cannot spread to other organs without progressing to the muscle layer first. Even though mine had not advanced to the muscle layer, she wanted to make sure it had not metastasized. The most common areas to find metastatic bladder cancer are the lungs, liver, and lymph nodes. These scans would hopefully verify that no cancer had developed in any of those organs. I also was going to start on BCG.

BCG is a three year regimen to treat non-muscle invasive bladder cancer. BCG is short for Bacillus Calmette-Guérin. It is a live strain of the TB virus (Mycobacterium bovis) that has been shown to decrease the likelihood of a recurrence of bladder cancer. It is an immunotherapy which means it boosts the body's immune system to fight off cancer. I would begin with the induction phase which is a once a week instillation directly into the bladder for six weeks. To avoid systemic complications, I had to heal from my second surgery, so I wouldn't start BCG until July 25th. After the six weeks, I would wait another six weeks for my bladder to recover from the irritation of the BCG, and then Dr. S would biopsy my bladder again to make sure there were no more cancer cells. If it was all clear, I would then progress to the maintenance phase of BCG. The maintenance phase is three weeks (instead of six) of weekly instillations of BCG after three months, six months, twelve months, eighteen months, twenty-four months, thirty months, and thirty-six months. In between, I would need cystoscopies to make sure no tumors were regenerating. The cystoscopies would be every three months for the first two years, every six months for the next two years, and then yearly after that for the rest of my life.

In the time between learning the results of the biopsy and beginning BCG treatment, I had the x-rays, CT scan, and MRI, and luckily no cancer was found. I researched what to expect with BCG treatment. I did consult "Dr. Google," as Dr. S would say, to determine the most common side effects. The most common side effects are fatigue, burning and urgency, blood and particles in the urine, fever, flu-like symptoms, nausea, vomiting, loss of appetite, headache, and dizziness. Great! Another treatment that may cause vomiting! I also read about how the treatment is given. One vial of BCG is mixed with fifty cubic centimeters of saline. It is then instilled into the bladder using a catheter. After instillation, I would be allowed to go home, but I would have to hold it for one hour. During that hour, I would have to lie for fifteen minutes each on my stomach, back, left side, and right side to make sure that the BCG reached all areas of the bladder. I refer to this as marinating! Then I would be permitted to go to the bathroom. Since BCG is a live virus, I would have to pour a cup of bleach into the toilet and let it sit there for fifteen minutes before flushing. I would need to do this every time I used the bathroom for the first six hours after the instillation to prevent contamination or spread.

Before BCG started, I visited Dr. R for a follow-up appointment. She had received my reports from Dr. S so she was well aware of my bladder cancer diagnosis. I confided in her that I was a little upset because Dr. S claimed that the Cytoxan from my breast cancer treatment could have caused the bladder cancer. Dr. R assured me that she had given me the smallest dose possible for the shortest length of time possible to still be effective. She insisted that the Cytoxan had not caused it, so I quipped, "I am just lucky to get cancer for the fourth time." We smiled, and she gave me a hug.

So it was just life as usual until July 25th.

On July 25th, I proceeded to Dr. S's office to receive my first BCG treatment. My appointment was scheduled for 9:45 in the morning. I decided not to eat or drink anything ahead of time. If I had to hold in the BCG, I didn't want it to be worse because I had had a lot to drink beforehand. I was feeling rather nervous because I didn't know exactly what to expect. After checking in and a short wait, the nurse called me back. She asked if this was my first BCG treatment, and when I said yes, she described what would happen each time. First, I would empty my bladder and leave a urine sample. She would test it to make sure I did not have an infection. If I did, I would not be allowed to have treatment that day. While she was testing my sample, I would wait in the exam room. If it tested infection free, she would come back and direct me to undress from the waist down while she went to prepare the BCG. Then I could cover up with the paper blanket and wait on the exam table for her to return. She would bring in the mixture and instill it into my bladder using a catheter. Afterwards, I could get dressed and go home.

Everything happened exactly as the nurse had described. I didn't have an infection so she brought in the BCG. Since it is a live virus, certain precautions have to be taken. Somewhat similar to the hazmat suit the doctor wore when I got I-131, she was well protected. She was dressed in her hospital scrubs and gloves like most medical professionals wear when they are seeing patients, but on her face she donned a mask with a plastic shield over it that covered her mouth, nose, and eyes. She was carrying a tiny vial containing the mixture which amazed me because I had thought it would be a lot more. It turns out that fifty cubic centimeters is only about one-fourth of a cup. It didn't seem like it would be too difficult to hold that for one hour, at least I thought so before it was in me! She swabbed my privates with antiseptic and inserted the catheter. Then she held up the vial to let gravity cause it to drip into me. I didn't expect to feel the liquid going in, but it felt cold. She informed me that they have to refrigerate the BCG so that was why it was cooler than room temperature. Surprisingly, it took only about two minutes for all of the liquid to drain from the vial and into me! She quickly cleaned up all of the tools (catheter, wipes, vial, extra pad she had placed under me to catch any drips, etc.) and instructed me to get dressed and head on home. Before leaving the room, she asked if I knew what to do when I got home. I replied that I had to marinate fifteen minutes on each side (stomach, back, left, and right) before emptying my bladder and that I had to pour bleach in the toilet and let it sit for fifteen minutes before flushing every time I went for the first six hours. She laughed at my use of the term "marinate" and decided that it sounded like I knew what to do. She emphasized that I should contact Dr. S's office if I developed flu-like symptoms or ran a fever over one hundred degrees.

When I returned to my apartment, it was only 10:30. I was stunned at how fast the whole process was. I proceeded to marinate. I decided I would lie on my stomach first. Nothing is worse than lying on your stomach when you really have to pee. I set the timer on my phone and was watching HGTV's "Love It or List It." When the timer went off, I decided to do my back next thinking that would be the second most uncomfortable position if I felt I really had to pee. After completing all four sides, I went to the bathroom. It was fairly painful, so I quickly poured in the bleach, set the timer for fifteen minutes, and went to get a drink to take the Uribel to help alleviate the feeling of burning and urgency. I remembered that Gatorade had been recommended to me during chemo so I had purchased some Gatorade to have on hand with the BCG treatments. I poured a big glass, took the medicine, and laid back down on the couch. I had taken the day off from work and didn't know how severe the side effects would be.

The side effects were manageable at first. I had the burning and urgency for about the first two hours. Then around 3:00 in the afternoon, I had an unusual sensation. It was kind of reminiscent of chemo brain.

My head felt heavy and my brain felt foggy. My eyes were stinging, and I felt a wave of fatigue. So this was the fatigue they were talking about! It's hard to describe. My body was so tired, but if I closed my eyes, I couldn't sleep. It wasn't that kind of tired. I felt like I had run a marathon and had a substantial weight on my chest. It was weird and fairly unpleasant. I also didn't like the mild eye stinging. Fortunately, by the end of the next day, the side effects had dissipated. I thought, "Okay, that wasn't so bad. I can do this five more times."

The next week's treatment was similar. There were only two differences. First, while I was under the paper blanket, a male nurse entered the room to administer the BCG. Before he started, he asked me if I would mind if he treated me or if I would prefer it to be a woman. Without blinking an eye, I responded that I didn't mind and that I didn't need a woman. At that point in my life, I had been poked, prodded, and examined by equally as many men as women, and I was no longer shy or modest. As it turned out, he has been the one to instill all but one of the following twenty-one treatments. He only missed one because he was on vacation. He is such a charming person, and as much as I am not fond of the treatment, I really enjoy seeing him and chatting with him at each appointment. The second difference was that the side effects lasted longer this time, for two more days.

All of the next four treatments were similar, with the side effects lasting about two to three days. The last treatment in the series was on August 29, 2016. Dr. S wanted to wait until October 10th to perform another bladder biopsy to verify that the BCG had eradicated of all of the cancer cells. She explained that it was important to wait six weeks for my bladder to heal from the BCG. BCG irritates the bladder, and if she did the biopsy too soon, it would look to her like my entire bladder was filled with cancer. Then she would call me back to her office on October 21st to discuss the results. So, I had another wait.

On October 21st, Dr. S did not deliver the best news. She reported that there were still CIS cells in my bladder. The BCG had not gotten rid of all of the cancer. I felt like I had failed a test. When I was in school, I had always been a good student and worked hard to get good grades. I think I even said to her that this is the first test I've ever failed in my life! She assured me that it isn't uncommon to have a second induction phase of BCG before moving on to the maintenance phase. She indicated that studies have shown that adding the drug Interferon to the BCG is an effective treatment if the first induction phase has failed. She clarified that it would be another six weeks of BCG with the Interferon mixed in starting November 7th. She warned me that Interferon causes the side effects of BCG to be worse. I thought, "Okay. I'm a warrior. I've prevailed so far, what's six more weeks?"

The six weeks of BCG with Interferon were not quite what I expected. I had assumed that the fatigue, burning, urgency, and eye stinging would all be stronger. That is not exactly what happened. Only the eye stinging increased. In fact, I went to an ophthalmologist because it turns out there is a rare side effect of BCG that causes eye problems. It figures that I would get that! I was given eye drops that felt good when I first used them, but didn't really alleviate the problem. If I was patient and waited a few days, the eye stinging went away. The rest of the side effects were not stronger, they just lasted longer and longer with each treatment – a week rather than just a few days. By the second to last one, I didn't have a chance to feel well before it was time for the last one.

One upsetting event occurred during the second induction phase. The third instillation was the one that I received when my usual male nurse was on vacation. A very pleasant female nurse informed me that she was covering for him while he was on vacation and that she usually worked at a different office. At the fifth treatment, Dr. S disclosed that the female nurse had just given me straight BCG and didn't mix in the Interferon. Dr. S believed that it wouldn't make a difference if I got six BCG treatments and only five mixed with the Interferon. She claimed that it would still have the same effectiveness. However, when I went home and thought about it, I decided I wanted to have a seventh dose so that I had the full six with the Interferon. Why? First of all, as with my breast cancer, I wanted to fight this disease with everything I've got. I wanted to make sure I got the most complete treatment. I don't ever want to look back and have any regrets that I didn't do everything in my power to fight this. Second of all, there are serious ramifications if the second induction phase is not successful in eradicating all of the cancer. If two induction phases have failed, the usual recommendation is to remove the bladder. I really, really, really want to keep my bladder. So, when I went back for the sixth treatment, I conveyed my thoughts to Dr. S. She consented and set up another appointment for the same time the following week. She also scheduled another bladder biopsy for February 13, 2017.

On February 13, 2017, I returned to the surgi-center for the bladder biopsy. I was extremely nervous. I wanted the BCG/Interferon mixture to be successful and prayed that it was. I was terrified that I was going to find out that I had to have my bladder removed. The surgery proceeded similarly to the last two biopsies until I woke up from the anesthesia. I was immediately in a great deal of discomfort. Supposedly, the anesthesiologist had put pain medication in my IV, but I felt immediate burning and urgency. When I went to the bathroom, it was that familiar but unwelcome feeling of peeing shards of glass. As it turned out, Dr. S later divulged that she had extracted many more samples of tissue this time, almost like cherry picking. She wanted to be certain that she explored every area of my bladder and could confidently report that I was cancer free if they all came back benign. So, in a way, I was relieved to have the pain because it meant I would have an accurate diagnosis.

My appointment to meet with Dr. S to discuss the results was scheduled for February 20th. She knew how anxious I was so she actually called me on the 17th. She was pleased to report that I was cancer free. I wanted to jump for joy, but she commented that there were abnormal cells. I wanted to question her more about that, but she suggested that we discuss it in person on the 20th. She emphasized that I should be happy that I was cancer free.

Abnormal cells? That's what I had right next to the cancer cells in my breast. Can I really be certain that I am cancer free?

Dr. S and I had a long discussion on February 20th. I confided in her that I was concerned because she had mentioned there were abnormal cells. She seemed to bristle as if I was questioning her expertise. I explained that I trusted her and was not questioning her expertise, but that I had had a bad experience with the biopsy results for my breast cancer. At first the pathologist had reported that he didn't see any cancer cells, just abnormal ones. Then a few days later when he reread the slides, he confirmed that there were cancer cells. After I described my prior experience, she visibly softened. She clarified that the abnormalities were changes due to the BCG and had nothing to do with cancer cells. The muscle layer tissue samples were all clear of cancer as well. Thank goodness. I was tremendously relieved and thrilled to be able to keep my bladder. I could now move on to the maintenance phase.

I was so excited to be cancer free that I went home and shared my good news on Facebook. I wrote, "My bladder cancer was tenacious but I am 'tenaciouser!' For the first time since May, I am cancer free!! Now I begin the maintenance phase – 'chemo' every three to six months for the next three years to keep me cancer free!"

So, as of this writing, I have completed my first three maintenance cycles of BCG (three, six, and twelve months). Unfortunately, the side effects can be cumulative. I have experienced fatigue, burning and urgency, eye stinging, headaches, and dizziness, all of which have been intense and worsen with each treatment. There was one cycle that I just couldn't hold the BCG in for the full hour. I felt like my bladder was going to burst! However, I am pleased to report that my last three cystoscopies have been clear of cancer. I also have had normal bloodwork and mammograms. It is an unbelievably wonderful feeling to be cancer free!

So, remember when I remarked that I never know what I'm looking at when I glance at the results of scans or x-rays? With each cystoscopy, Dr. S takes four pictures of the inside of my bladder. She prints them out on one piece of paper and always makes an extra copy for me to keep. After one of the cystoscopies, I was waiting in her office to chat with her and noticed the picture laying on her desk. I picked it up, and as I was looking at it, she walked into the room. I was trying to make sense of what I was seeing, and she quietly reached over, grasped the photo, and inverted it. I had been looking at it upside down, and she turned it the right way! I had no idea!

Part 2

Be Your Own Best Advocate

The first thing cancer taught me is you must be your own best advocate. It is imperative that you are. No one knows your body better than you do. If you notice something, don't wait. Check with your doctor right away. Like they say at the airport, "If you see something, say something!" Some people are afraid to consult their doctor because they are worried about what the doctor might find, yet studies show that treatments are more effective in patients who take an active role in their healthcare. A patient who does not speak up or is passive is less likely to get well (Downs).

Early detection is key. In many cases, the sooner cancer is diagnosed and treated, the better a person's chance for a full recovery. When cancer is detected at an earlier stage, before it has metastasized or gotten too large, it can often be easily surgically removed or treated. The affected organ can be preserved and the need for treatments like chemotherapy can be unnecessary, thus avoiding the side effects of chemo. Some cancers respond better when the treatment is started early. Early detection can be the difference between life and death ("The Importance of Early Detection")!

With all of my cancers, I contacted my doctor right away when I noticed a change in my body. I'd rather err on the side of caution and hopefully have it turn out to be nothing, than ignore something that could be serious.

When I noticed a lump in my neck, I arranged for the soonest possible appointment with my doctor. My thyroid cancer was followed and treated. The tumor was only seven millimeters in size. Who knows how large it could have grown or what complications it could have caused had I waited.

When I observed a change in the shape of my left breast on a Saturday, I made an appointment with my doctor the following Monday. That tumor was only one centimeter. It wasn't seen on a mammogram, and it wasn't felt on a physical examination. Since I only receive mammograms yearly, if I wouldn't have mentioned anything, how many years would have transpired before it was noticed? Who knows how large it could have grown or if it would have metastasized elsewhere in my body.

When I discovered blood in the toilet one evening, I saw my doctor the next day. The tumor had not spread to the muscle layer. As I mentioned earlier, one of my philosophies is never stop learning. So, after each cancer diagnosis, I would research and try to become knowledgeable about that type of cancer. After reading about bladder cancer, I found out that the most common first sign is visible blood in urine. I also discovered that many people ignore it because it usually goes away. That is what happened to me. By the next day, I no longer saw the blood. As I researched further, I learned that eventually the bleeding returns. However, who knows how much larger or deeper a tumor could grow in the meantime.

To this day, I cannot go to the bathroom without checking the toilet afterwards to make sure there is no blood. If I ever notice any, I will definitely contact Dr. S immediately!

I had a minor scare recently that actually turned out to be funny. Early one morning, I visited my dentist for my semi-annual appointment, and the hygienist informed me that she was going to take a panoramic x-ray of my teeth. Afterwards, I asked if I could see the film. It was obvious where my teeth were so she was pointing out my sinuses, nerves, jawbone, etc. Then she noticed a white spot that appeared to be in my upper spine in my neck. She exclaimed that she didn't know what it was and would ask the dentist. The dentist took one look and asked if I had ever had back surgery. I never have. He reported that it looked like it could be pins or screws. Since that wasn't it, he thought that maybe it was a calcification. He was going to confer with a dental colleague because he had never seen anything like it before. He handed me a copy of the x-ray before I left. As I started fearing the worst, cancer number five, it didn't help that I had been suffering with an ache in my neck for the past few days. I had thought it was a pulled muscle, but now I was not convinced. Luckily, I had both my cystoscopy with Dr. S and my checkup with Dr. R scheduled for the next week. I went to work and tried to keep my mind off my neck. I did check with "Dr. Google" during my lunch break and discovered that bone cancer does appear as white spots on x-rays and that a common location to find a metastasis of all three of my cancers (thyroid, breast, and bladder) was the bone! Great! As I was driving home from work, I had a thought. I hadn't removed my hearing aids for the x-ray. Could that be what had shown up on the film? I was still definitely going to show the picture to both Dr. S and Dr. R, but now I wasn't quite as worried. It was probably my hearing aids. The soreness in my neck went away over the weekend. It was a relief not only to no longer have the pain, but also because it allowed me to be cautiously optimistic that the spot on the film was my hearing aids. Sure enough, I presented the x-ray to Dr. S on Monday, and she stated that it was definitely my hearing aids. Even though I have implicit faith in Dr. S, to be extra prudent, I showed it to Dr. R on Wednesday, and she concurred that it was my hearing aids. She remarked that nothing else looks like that. No cancer! No metastasis! Phew!

Doctors don't refer to cancer as being "cured" because undetected cancer cells can remain in the body after treatment. These undetected cells can cause a recurrence later. Instead, the preferred description is no evidence of disease (NED) or clear/normal/benign scans and bloodwork. My last thyroid blood test was normal. My last mammogram was benign. As long as the BCG keeps doing the trick and I don't have a recurrence, I am NED for bladder cancer. All of my cystoscopies have been clear with no evidence of disease. My prognosis is excellent according to both Dr. S and Dr. R. I believe I owe this to the fact that I was my own best advocate and pro-active in getting medical help as soon as possible after I noticed a problem and to the excellent professional treatment I received from all of my doctors!

Never Lose Your Sense of Humor and Keep a Positive Attitude

The second thing cancer taught me is to never lose my sense of humor and keep a positive attitude. I think I have a decent sense of humor, and I've always been a positive and upbeat person. I don't and won't let cancer change that.

Experts say that laughter is the best medicine. Research has proven that there are many physical health benefits of laughter. It has been shown to lower stress hormones. When you laugh, you release endorphins which are the body's natural feel-good chemicals. When endorphins are released, you feel less stress and pain. Laughter also increases immune cells which are infection–fighting antibodies. This can help you ward off illnesses. A good laugh relieves physical tension and stress which can relax your muscles for up to forty-five minutes. Laughing for just ten to fifteen minutes burns about forty calories! When you laugh, blood flow is increased which can prevent heart attacks and strokes (Robinson et al).

In addition to these physical benefits, there are emotional benefits of laughter. Laughing eases anxiety, tension, and stress. It's hard to feel anxious or tense while you're laughing. Laughter adds joy and zest to life. It's contagious. If you hear someone else laugh, you are apt to join in. Therefore, your mood will improve. It has also been shown to improve mental functioning and self-esteem. Laughter enhances resilience (Robinson et al). It's amazing to me how many health benefits there are!

I am Ellen DeGeneres's biggest fan. Her. Biggest. Fan. She possesses all of the qualities that I admire in a person. She is kind, funny generous, loves animals, and cares about the environment. She is an inspiration. I strive to be like her. I record her show and watch it every day. For two years, I entered my information into her website every day to try to score tickets to a taping. Miraculously, I procured two tickets for the January 7, 2013 show. Valerie and I flew to L.A. for the weekend with the taping on Monday. It was one of the best experiences of my life! In the gift shop, I bought Ellen underwear, a t-shirt, and sweatpants. For every single doctor's appointment, scan, or treatment since then, I have sported all of my Ellen wear for good luck. I even purchased two small plush toys – one of Dory and one of Nemo. They fit in the palm of my hands. During every BCG treatment and every cystoscopy, I have gripped Dory in my right hand and Nemo in my left. They are my talismen! During scans where I am not permitted to hold them in my hands (MRIs or CT scans), I keep them in my purse so I know they are with me. *The Ellen DeGeneres Show* used to be televised in the late morning. When I scheduled my chemo treatments, I purposely arranged them with the show in mind. I scheduled chemo first thing in the morning so that I would be done in time to come home and watch her show "live." Even though the chemo made me feel ill, during that hour, I could forget about my troubles. Laughter truly is the best medicine because I would laugh during that hour, and it made me feel better. I even felt well enough to dance with her each time she danced after her monologue. Thank you Ellen for inspiring me and supporting me through my cancers!

I remember a time when laughter had a pronounced effect. I was in the midst of chemo treatment and there was a day when I felt awful. The "chemo brain" sensation was intense. A friend that I hadn't heard from in a long time called me to find out how I was doing. I didn't really have the strength to chat, but since I hadn't talked to her in a long time, I decided I would make it a quick call. I am so thankful I did. I don't remember exactly what she said, but we both started laughing. It was as if a switch had flipped! I immediately felt infinitely better. I was stunned at how just laughing made such an obvious difference. I'll never forget that.

I have always been a positive and optimistic person. I am not a big complainer and try to stay upbeat. I think that those qualities have also contributed to my prognosis. Research has shown that like laughter, having a positive, confident, cheery, and optimistic attitude has similar benefits.

The health benefits of a positive attitude are "increased life span, lower rates of depression, lower levels of distress, greater resistance to the common cold, better psychological and physical well-being, better cardiovascular health and reduced risk of death from cardiovascular disease, [and] better coping skills during hardships and times of stress" ("Positive Thinking: Stop Negative Self-Talk to Reduce Stress").

I am a firm believer that what happens in your brain (how you think and react to things) influences your body.

In addition to health benefits, there are other advantages to having a positive attitude. Thinking positively attracts favorable events. An upbeat attitude leads to improved relationships so you will increase your circle of friends and have more meaningful relationships. Cheery people make better first impressions. One key to success is having a positive attitude. By being positive, you will notice the good things in your life which will lead to a sense of peace and happiness. A confident attitude increases motivation. Optimistic thinking will make you look more beautiful. Now, who doesn't want to look more beautiful???!!! People who are happy, friendly, and smiling appear to be very attractive. Their inner beauty shines and becomes outwardly noticeable ("10 Benefits of Positive Thinking").

I'd certainly like to glean all of these benefits just from laughing and staying positive. I'd rather achieve these results from glee and optimism than from having to take medication to attain the same outcome.

I've heard that many more muscles are used to frown than to smile. So with little effort, smiling every day can lead to excellent physical and mental health and well-being. Also, laughing and keeping a positive attitude can help make the cancer journey more bearable.

With the Love and Support of Family, Friends, and Community, You Can Make it Through Anything!

The third thing cancer taught me is that with the love and support of family, friends, and community, you can make it through anything. I was overwhelmed by the outpouring of love and support I received. There were the responses one would expect: cards, phone calls, emails, texts, and hugs every day from family, friends, and neighbors. After hearing about any of my cancer diagnoses or while I was undergoing treatment, many people brought me chocolate because they know how much I love it. Maybe the title of this chapter should be "With the Love and Support of Family, Friends, and Community, and WITH CHOCOLATE, You Can Make it Through Anything!"

Here's a brief story to illustrate how much I love chocolate. When I was in high school, my hearing was tested. An audiogram was performed as part of a routine screening, and it showed that I possessed a congenital hearing loss in both ears. For many years, annual rechecks were conducted, and it was determined that the loss was degenerative. In my early thirties (right before my cancer journey began), I was fitted for hearing aids in both ears. As my doctor was discussing my options, he mentioned that there is a correlation between hearing loss and caffeine. He explained that studies have shown that higher amounts of caffeine can cause hearing to deteriorate. He asked me about my caffeine intake. I responded that I don't drink much coffee and that when I drink soda, I drink caffeine-free. He then added, "What about chocolate?" I remember my exact words to him were, "I'm going to be deaf!"

When I was diagnosed with breast cancer, the phone rang all the time. So many people wanted to know how I was doing. It was sometimes difficult to talk. Discussing what was happening made me re-live it. Often, I had to retell the same story many times a day. Sometimes, that was emotionally too difficult. There were occasions I just couldn't talk about it. When the phone rang, caller ID would announce who was calling. I would listen to who it was and decide whether I had the energy to speak with that person or not. If I didn't, I would signal to my husband by shaking my head no. He would then field the call for me and tell the person I was resting or couldn't talk. We used to joke that he was my bulldog.

There were also many examples that went above and beyond. I felt tremendously blessed and loved. I will try to describe all of them and hopefully not leave any out. If you are reading this, and something you did is not mentioned, please know that it is not because it was not appreciated. I may have some residual chemo brain which has affected my memory!

As I've expressed several times, waiting for test results is one of the worst parts of cancer. When Dr. W had assured me that I would get the results from the breast biopsy by Wednesday, and I still hadn't heard by Thursday, my sisters and parents were as nervous and anxious as I was. Lori sent me a bouquet of flowers with a note that read, "Thinking of you. Love you." It was very sweet and thoughtful. I remember Lani asking why Aunt Lori had sent me flowers. Since I hadn't revealed to Lani what was happening yet, I answered that Aunt Lori wanted to cheer me up because she knew I was having a stressful week. It was the truth, maybe not the whole truth, but nonetheless, the truth. I have always felt that I would never lie to my children. I remember that after I disclosed to Lani that I had breast cancer, she remarked, "So that's why Aunt Lori sent you flowers!"

When I was being treated with chemotherapy in 2007, Lani was in high school and Valerie was in middle school. I was the family member who usually prepared dinner. Betsy organized meals for us so that I wouldn't have to worry about cooking. She guaranteed that every Monday and Tuesday of chemo weeks, there was a full meal for four people delivered to us that needed little or no preparation. Heating it up in the oven or microwave was all that was necessary. These dinners were made by friends and neighbors. One of the neighbors had only recently moved into the neighborhood! I was extremely touched.

When I was experiencing the induction phases of BCG, again my friends provided me with meals. Some of the friends were the same ones who had done this before, and some were other or new friends I had made. My friend Allison gathered the ingredients to make a meal and delivered them to my apartment. She proceeded to cook dinner and we ate together. I remember it being quite an enjoyable evening.

The Avon Walk used to be a two day walk of 39.3 miles (26.2 which is a full marathon on day one and 13.1 which is a half marathon on day two). Walkers would solicit sponsors, and the contributions would be donated to the fight against breast cancer. The money could be targeted for research or to directly help patients. Walkers could opt to camp overnight in tents after day one, at a location determined by Avon, or they could go home or to a hotel and return to start the walk on day two. In 2007, the year I was being treated with chemotherapy for breast cancer, Avon chose the school where I worked as the campsite. The art teacher decided to create a project with the students in my honor and in recognition of Avon's election to be there. She did not share what was happening, but explained to me that there was an event at the school one night and I needed to attend. I donned one of my hats to match my outfit and cover my bald head, and drove to school. I hadn't been there for several weeks, so it felt strange to walk in the door. I was ushered into the gym where there were bleachers assembled. Many students and parents were already seated. The art teacher picked up the microphone and revealed that they were conducting a fundraiser for Avon in my honor. I was so touched that I cried! The students had designed pink clay shoes as a project. The art teacher made one as an example that she presented to me. It is hanging in my kitchen today. She also cut out footprints on pink paper and asked the students to write well wishes to me on them. They were hung on a large piece of bulletin board paper that was displayed so that the Avon walkers would see it. Reading what was written on the footprints made me cry again. The students were so sweet. They wrote "We miss you." "Get well soon." "Stay strong!" "You can beat this!" The art teacher persuaded some eighth grade boys to wear pink bandanas and pink shirts, in my honor, and dish out ice cream. I never would have thought that eighth grade boys would ever want to be seen wearing pink, and here were these macho boys wearing pink because of me! They were so excited to see me and to serve me ice cream. The money they collected from the sale of the ice cream was donated to Avon. The art teacher also created a dream catcher for me using pink beads, pink leather strips, and pink feathers. It has been hanging from the rearview mirror in my car ever since. It was a wonderful evening, one that I will never forget.

My parents are "snowbirds." They have a condo in Milwaukee very close to the house where I grew up. They also have a condo in Delray Beach, Florida. They spend the winter months in Florida because Wisconsin winters are very brutal! Yet, even though my parents live far from me, every time I had surgery they came to stay with me for at least a week. When I had the breast biopsy, it was scheduled for the Monday after Thanksgiving. My parents had come for the holiday and their return flight was scheduled for that day. As soon as they found out about my procedure, they called the airline and rescheduled their flight for the day after my biopsy so that they could accompany me to the procedure. Also, I vividly remember our conversation after my first cystoscopy that revealed the tumor. After leaving Dr. S's office on a Friday knowing that I would have the surgery on Tuesday, I stumbled to my car, sat in the driver's seat, and withdrew my cellphone from my purse. I called my parents. They both picked up the phone simultaneously because they had been awaiting my call and were praying for good news. They asked what the doctor said. I replied, "It's not good news." My mother immediately responded, "We will come to be with you." Each time my mother stayed with me she would cook and prepare meals, do laundry, and help in any way she could so that I could focus on healing. I have the best parents!

When Dr. S first explained the details of BCG treatment to me, I was overwhelmed. If all went as scheduled, I would receive twenty-seven treatments! (As it turns out, I will have a total of thirty-four because of the extra seven due to the BCG/Interferon second induction phase). I was lamenting on the phone to a cousin that I was having a hard time seeing the light at the end of the tunnel. She made an excellent suggestion. She recommended that I make a chart and check off each treatment after I complete it. That's exactly what I did! The chart is titled "Kicking Cancer's Butt" above the check-off boxes. As daunting as thirty-four boxes look on the chart, it is an immense feeling of gratification to put an "X" in a box when I finish marinating! I am grateful to my cousin for suggesting this! As of this writing, there are twenty-two boxes checked.

When I was diagnosed with bladder cancer, I was living by myself. My sister, Jill, did not want me to be alone for the first six of my BCG treatments. She would drive over to my apartment to pick me up, escort me to and from treatment, and stay with me long enough to make sure that I had lunch and dinner, both of which she prepared. The few times that she was not able to be with me because she was visiting her daughter, son-in-law, and grandson, her dear friend Laura (who has become my close friend as well) took her place. When I needed the second round of BCG treatments mixed with Interferon, Jill was concerned because Dr. S claimed the side effects would be worse. So, not only did she repeat what she had done for the first six treatments, but she also slept over on the nights of treatment to make sure that I was okay. Even though I don't mind going alone, it was very comforting to have company and to have meals prepared. Not only didn't I need to plan the meals, but I didn't need to prepare them or clean up after them either! What a blessing!

When I was hospitalized for the I-131 treatment, visitors were not encouraged. Jill insisted she wanted to come. The room was shaped like a long rectangle with the bed on one short end and the door to the room at the other short end. A chair was positioned by the door. No one was allowed to come any closer than the chair. This was the precaution they insisted upon to prevent exposure to radiation. Jill sat in the chair, and we chatted across the distance. She was the only visitor I had for the three days in the hospital.

While undergoing chemo, I was surfing the Internet one day. I stumbled upon a website called *Cancer Survivor's Network*. It is designed with links to different types of cancer. When you click on a link, it takes you to a discussion board where people can pose questions about what they're experiencing, and other people can answer. The questions are organized by thread so you can search for a specific topic to read about it. I frequently read what others wrote and posted a few questions of my own. The responses people gave were tremendously supportive. Most people who answered had been through a similar experience so they were extremely empathetic. I found it helpful to read about other people encountering similar situations and circumstances as mine. I realized I was not alone. That was exceptionally comforting.

At my appointment with Dr. S when she confirmed that I did have bladder cancer, she presented me with binder similar to the one I received from Dr. W when I was diagnosed with breast cancer. In addition to containing information that answered every question I had about bladder cancer, the binder included a pamphlet describing a website called *Bladder Cancer Advocacy Network* (BCAN). BCAN is similar to *Cancer Survivor's Network*, but only focuses on bladder cancer. It was from that website that I gleaned a great deal of information about what to expect from BCG treatments. One person wrote about the fear of recurrence. Another person responded and said that he or she (I wish I could remember who it was) had coined the term "scanxiety" to mean the fear of the results of an upcoming scan. I can totally relate! The most wonderful posts are when people share good news about clear scans or making it two, three, five, or more years with no recurrence. NED (no evidence of disease) are a cancer survivor's favorite words to hear! The responses flood in with congratulations and celebratory wishes. It's a community that no one wants to be a part of because that means they've had cancer, yet it's a community comprised of a tremendous amount of love and support!

You never know where you might meet someone who becomes a dear friend. Often it's a very unlikely place. Soon after I moved to Maryland, I joined a Jazzercise class where I met Amy. She and I have been friends ever since. About eight years ago, Amy wanted to organize a group of women who would enjoy meeting once a month to dine out, so what I like to refer to as my "ladies group" was born. My "ladies group" consists of Amy, Debi, Shari, Joy, and me. We have been going to dinner monthly for the last eight years. Every time we meet, the conversation is non-stop. We share both exciting and sad events in our lives. They have been the most wonderful women to have in my life. So many times they have lifted my spirits when I expressed my fears or discomfort about what I was undergoing.

When I was diagnosed with bladder cancer, I bought three car magnets. If you look at the back of my car, not only will you see a Packers and Brewers sticker (I love my Milwaukee sports teams), but you will also see three cancer ribbons. There is a ribbon for each cancer I've had: thyroid, breast, and bladder.

At my most recent dinner with my "ladies group," I shared that I had "scanxiety" about a cystoscopy scheduled for the next day as part of my ongoing follow-up treatment. Shari remarked, "It's going to go well. No more ribbons!"

Debi has given me numerous gifts. She has treated me to coffee at Starbucks more times than I can count. She has presented me with several cat-themed trinkets. She also gave me a heart-shaped rock with the word "strength" chiseled in it. All of these gifts are on display in my corner curio cabinet. She frequently tells me that she is always thinking of me which warms my heart.

My friend Michelle has been a big emotional support. She was also diagnosed with bladder cancer. Hers was low grade, discovered about fifteen years ago, and treated with BCG. She, more than anyone else, understands what I have experienced, even though she was lucky to have had very few side effects from the BCG. We often share our thoughts, fears, and experiences. I hope that I'm equally as supportive of her as she is of me.

Lani and Valerie have been considerably sweet throughout my cancer journey. Even with their busy lives, they make time to check in on me, especially on days I've had treatment. They write me notes, cards, or post on Facebook. What they write is always extremely touching. Valerie said that I'm incredible, I am her rock and her inspiration, and that I'm the strongest person she has ever known. Lani said that I am her hero! On my birthday one year, Lani posted,

"Cheers to another year of resilience, strength, and happiness. Love you!"

When I update Facebook with the latest news regarding my treatment, I get the most supportive comments. One friend called me a "trooper survivor!" Another friend wrote, "You are such an inspiration with your positive attitude. Stay strong!" Betsy said, "You have a wonderful perspective on a difficult treatment. You rock!" Several people told me to "Kick cancer's butt!" Many more wrote, "Sending hugs!" A fellow cancer survivor added, "You are an amazing ambassador for survivors!" A teacher I used to work with wrote, "You are truly a great model of strength for others who are facing this diagnosis." One of the first friends I made when I moved to Maryland was Jan. She and I were both hired to teach for our first year at the same school. We commiserated about our principal who was a nightmare. We were so close that she even made the trip to Milwaukee for my wedding. On my birthday, the day after my bladder cancer surgery, Jan wrote the following post: "In dancing ....they begin with 5, 6, 7, 8........you are 56.....no matter the challenge you seem (like Ellen) to dance through with strength and determination. This birthday is a tough one.....but I have every confidence you will be on your toes and face the music and DANCE through and be rather awesome. Because you are." Just thinking about what people have posted brings tears to my eyes! There are so many more, but it would take a whole book just to list them all!

The friends I have known the longest are Ianne and her younger sister, Mari. We met when I was in second or third grade and grew up around the corner from each other. We could visit each other by walking all around the block, or we could take a shortcut that we called "cutting through the woods." At the end of my back yard, there was a narrow strip of wooded area that was about twenty feet wide and spanned a couple of blocks in length. I would cross that, cut across a neighbor's back and front lawn to the road, and Ianne's and Mari's house was on the other side of the street. Ianne still lives in the neighborhood in which we grew up, and Mari moved to Chicago. In spite of the distance between us, we still keep in touch as often as possible given our busy lives. During all of my cancers, both Ianne and Mari would regularly call or text to inquire how I was doing. They each said that they wished they lived closer so that they could be with me in person for more support. Although that would be fantastic, just hearing their voices or reading their texts did wonders to lift my spirits. We share such a long history that every time we talk, it's as if no time has passed since the last time, even if it has been a few months.

Dr. R has a therapist in her office named D. I have been seeing her for many years, and she has been incredibly helpful. D only works with cancer patients and their caregivers. She understands the unique fears of cancer survivors, and often congratulates me on how well I continue to deal with my situation. I tell her that it is in large part because of her, and she contends that it is primarily because of me and who I am inside.

I cannot say that I do it alone. I have a huge network of family and friends who show me more love and support than I ever thought was possible!

I Am Stronger Than I Ever Thought Possible

The last thing cancer taught me is that I am stronger than I ever thought possible. Cancer is an all-encompassing disease. It affects the body both physically and emotionally. The physical effects are not just the disease itself. There are many tests done to diagnose cancer that are painful. Many of the treatments are also uncomfortable. I can honestly say that I have been poked and prodded in more places in my body and more times than I can count. Many cancer patients have scars from surgeries where tumors were removed. In some cases, these scars can be disfiguring or ugly, especially if they are located in a place not covered by clothing. Fortunately for me, my scars have all healed nicely and aren't too noticeable. I look at them as medals of honor and bravery for battles I have fought and won!

The emotional effects of cancer start at the first sign that anything is wrong. First, there is the worry about what the results of the biopsy or other diagnostic tests will be. Then there is the stress about what treatment will be like. Will it be painful? Will it make me sick? Next come the fears about what the prognosis will be. Cancer used to be a death sentence. Thankfully, with the advances made in medical diagnosis and treatment, that is no longer the only outcome.

All of the effects, both physical and emotional, are long lasting. Some radiation treatments cause permanent physical damage to the body that can affect a person for the rest of his or her life. Once diagnosed with cancer, it is common to go through post-traumatic stress disorder (PTSD). Many cancer patients never stop worrying about a recurrence. I always get nervous before my mammograms, cystoscopies, and blood tests because I never want to hear the words, "You have cancer" spoken to me again in my lifetime. It's "scanxiety!" I have lived through these physical and emotional events four times. Even so, as difficult as it has been, I have never felt that I can't handle it. I haven't particularly enjoyed it, but it is part of my life's journey and I wouldn't change it if I could because look what I've learned!

Even though I try to remain strong, I have experienced moments of weakness, many of them. I wept when I thought my voice therapy was not helping. At one point during chemotherapy when I was feeling very ill, I cried. Once when I looked in the mirror and saw my bald head, I sobbed, mourning the loss of my hair. There were times when I asked, "Why me?" or complained that life wasn't fair. Cancer is an awful disease that causes a tremendous amount of suffering for both the patient and his or her loved ones. I've lost relatives and pets to this disease. Both of my grandparents on my mother's side died from cancer. The cat who had trouble adjusting to going back to the house, died in 2017 at the age of twelve from intestinal cancer. One of my other cats was diagnosed with lung cancer just as I was putting the finishing touches on this memoir. He is thirteen. He is my baby. I am so sad to know that I am going to lose him soon to this dreaded disease! I have a friend who has a chronic illness that causes a lot of pain, numbness, and tingling when she has flare-ups. There are times when she feels so depressed that she sets a timer for fifteen minutes and allows herself to cry for just that amount of time. After the fifteen minutes, she dries her eyes and carries on as if nothing just happened. I never set a timer, but I also try not to wallow in self-pity. I only allow these moments of despair, sadness, or depression to be fleeting. I don't dwell on them. A good cry, long enough to get it out of my system, actually helps me feel stronger and rejuvenated. Overall my life is full and I am blessed to be surrounded by wonderful people and to feel well on most days.

Around the time of my third cancer diagnosis, I was reading a book called Change of Heart by Jodi Piccoult, who is one of my favorite authors. She started every chapter with a quote by a famous person. There was one by Mother Teresa that resonated with me. I am paraphrasing it here, but it said something like, "I know G-d will only give me what he knows I can handle. I just wish he didn't trust me so much!" I think that is how every cancer patient feels. Cancer is a lot to handle, but I did it four times, and here I am!

Music gives me strength. There is nothing better than belting out an inspirational song at the top of my lungs in my flat and off-key voice. I still don't know where Valerie got her angelic singing voice because it certainly wasn't from me! There are countless songs about strength and courage in the face of adversity. Here are fifteen of my favorites:

1. "Hero" by Mariah Carey
2. "Fight Song" by Rachel Plattten
3. "Stronger" by Kelly Clarkson
4. "Brave" by Sara Bereilles
5. "Fighter" by Christina Aguilera
6. "Rise" by Katy Perry
7. "Firework" by Katy Perry
8. "When You Believe" by Whitney Houston and Mariah Carey
9. "Survivor" by Destiny's Child
10. "The Climb" by Miley Cyrus
11. "Don't Stop Believing" by Journey
12. "It's My Life" by Bon Jovi
13. "Shake it Off" by Taylor Swift
14. "Go the Distance" by Michael Bolton from Disney's movie "Hercules"
15. "Eye of the Tiger" by Survivor

As I typed these, I was fascinated to notice that the majority of them are by women. Women are warriors!

I will never forget something my friend Joy said to me. About a week after my first TURBT, Joy and I were sitting together at a luncheon to celebrate the engagement of the daughter of our friend, Shari. I had driven my parents to the airport after they had stayed with me following the TURBT, and then from the airport, I had continued on to the luncheon. I told Joy that I had just been diagnosed with cancer for the fourth time. Her response was, "Sue, cancer picked the wrong woman to mess with!" I loved that! I always want to be that woman.

Cancer empowered me. I used to be very shy and avoid confrontation. Although I still don't really enjoy it, I am more apt to speak up and have overcome my shyness. I also have become more proactive in the fight against cancer by becoming involved in numerous cancer fundraising events. In 2005, Betsy informed me that a friend of hers was the captain of a Relay for Life team. Relay for Life is sponsored by the American Cancer Society. It was conceived by a doctor who asked people to donate money to sponsor him for walking around a track for twenty-four hours. His thinking was that cancer doesn't sleep, so he wouldn't either for one day. He donated the money that he received to the American Cancer Society and hence, Relay for Life was born. Now, at least one member from each team must walk the track at all times during the twenty-four hours. The teams set up campsites around the track to spend the night, sleeping in shifts. All participants fundraise. I joined Betsy's friend's team and had a fabulous experience. For five years after that, I was the captain of my own Relay for Life team which I named the Chocoholics (I'm sure you can guess why)! Twice I spoke at the survivor luncheon held at the beginning of the event. That was a true testament to overcoming my shyness. My speech was a condensed version of this memoir. I also participated in the Avon Walk for Breast Cancer after five years of survivorship and again after ten years of survivorship. In total, I have raised over ten thousand dollars in the fight against cancer. It is my hope that one day soon we will live in a world where there is no such thing as cancer, or if it is diagnosed, there is a one hundred percent successful cure every time.

Conclusion

So, even though it's been a long and often painful journey, I feel lucky to have had cancer four times. Each time, cancer taught me something new and important about life.

Cancer changed my outlook and helped me learn what is really important - family and friends! I will always make time to be with the people I hold dear. Everything else will always come second. My family and friends were there for me when I needed them most and I will never forget that. I want them to know how incredibly thankful I am and how blessed I feel. I want them to feel the same way from me.

Cancer taught me to take time to enjoy life. It reminded me to continue to pursue the things I enjoy doing. I am a member of two different book clubs. Each one meets about once every four to six weeks. I'm also a member of two different Bunco groups, playing once a month with each group. In addition, I'm involved with six meet-up groups. These groups get together to hike, visit museums, go out to dinner, go to shows, etc. I keep busy doing what I enjoy. Oprah Winfrey says, "Live your best life." That is exactly what I try to do every day. As my favorite fish, Dory says, I'm going to "just keep swimming" with dignity and grace!

I'm not a gambler, but I do try to win prizes on occasion, and I never do. I've tried my luck with sweepstakes, raffles, Bingo, and the lottery when it is mega-millions, but to no avail. Recently, there was a raffle at my hair salon and I was hoping to win a hair dryer because mine is on its last legs. After the drawing, I was complaining to Michelle that as usual, my name wasn't picked. I commented that I wasn't surprised though because I never win anything. But then I paused for a moment and thought, "I am winning at life. I may not have won any money or material objects, but I am alive. I've had cancer four times, yet here I am – alive. Yes, I am winning at life!" I guess that's my positive attitude shining through!

There is a famous quote that says, "When something bad happens, you have three choices: you can let it define you, you can let it destroy you, or you can let it strengthen you." I chose to let cancer strengthen me! I am a warrior! Cancer taught me to be my own best advocate; to maintain my sense of humor and positive attitude; to recognize that with the love and support of family, friends, and community I can make it through anything; and to stay strong. Because of this, I am, and always will be a survivor!

Works Cited

"Cancer-The Importance of Early Detection." *Herzliya Medical Center*, 10 May 2015, www.hmcisrael.com/news/cancer-importance-early-detection-2015-05-10.

Downs, Martin. "Be Your Own Health Advocate." *WebMD*, www.webmd.com/healthy-aging/features/be-your-own-health-advocate#1.

"How is Chemotherapy Given?" *Breastcancer.org*, 5 Mar. 2015, www.breastcancer.org/treatment/chemotherapy/process/how.

"Positive Thinking: Stop Negative Self-Talk to Reduce Stress." *Mayo Clinic*, 18 Feb. 2017, www.mayoclinic.org/healthy-lifestyle/stress-management/in-depth/positive-thinking/art-20043950.

Robinson, Lawrence, et al. "Laughter is the Best Medicine." *Helpguide.org*, Mar. 2018, www.helpguide.org/articles/mental-health/laughter-is-the-best-medicine.htm.

"10 Benefits of Positive Thinking." *Beauty and Tips Magazine*, www.beautyandtips.com/motivation/10-benefits-of-positive-thinking/.

Acknowledgements

Special thanks to Debi Stuart for editing my first draft and to Jill Bederman for her input and suggestions on polishing the final draft.

Thank you again to everyone mentioned in this book for your endless love and support as I have traveled this journey.

75272150R00073

Made in the USA
Middletown, DE
04 June 2018